THE FAMILY TENNIS BOOK

BY JOHN AND ANGIE NEWCOMBE

THE FAMILY TENNIS BOOK

BY JOHN AND ANGIE NEWCOMBE

with CLARENCE MABRY

Photographs by MELCHIOR DIGIACOMO
Illustrations by DICK KOHFIELD

A Delta Special

ACKNOWLEDGEMENTS

A DELTA SPECIAL

Published by
Dell Publishing Co., Inc.
1 Dag Hammarskjold Plaza
New York, New York 10017

Delta ® TM 755118, Dell Publishing Co., Inc.

Reprinted by arrangement with
Tennis Magazine, A New York Times Company,
297 Westport Avenue,
Norwalk, Connecticut 06856.
Quadrangle/The New York Times Book Co.
10 East 53 Street
New York, New York 10022.

Printed in the United States of America
First Delta printing—May 1976

Writing a book has never been a driving ambition in my life. I'm your basic tennis player, and about all I've ever wanted was to be the best tennis player in the world. So when Asher Birnbaum, publisher, and Bill Davis, president, of *Tennis* magazine, suggested that I write a book, I told them I wasn't really interested. But, the more I thought about it, the more I liked the idea because I realized I would like to do a book on family tennis. Playing tennis with my own family has always meant a great deal to me and it's a subject I'm very interested in.

It would be difficult with my heavy tournament schedule to write all of it myself, but luckily there was an ideal choice as coauthor, Clarence Mabry, my close friend and business partner at the T Bar M Tennis Ranch in New Braunfels, Tex. Clarence is one of America's top teaching pros and is a former tournament player himself. For many years he coached the Trinity (Texas) University team that produced such fine players as Chuck McKinley, Frank Froehling, Dick Stockton and Brian Gottfried. He presently coaches the Houston E-Z Riders of World Team Tennis. Clarence and I have worked together for several years conducting clinics for young people and adults and he knows and shares my ideas about teaching tennis. He spent numerous weeks developing the concept of the book and worked long hours with the editors. His patient and unselfish contributions have meant a great deal to me and to this book.

Another who shares my feeling about the family aspects of tennis is my wife Angie, a fine amateur player before we were married. Because so much of our family life revolves around tennis, ideas in the book are really based on our experiences together as a tennis family. So, although the book is written in the first person singular, there is a lot of Angie in it, too. She also wrote many of the photographic captions and both she and the children helped out by posing for the pictures. I'd like to acknowledge the tennis staff at the T Bar M Ranch who have worked with our teaching methods.

Ordinarily, sports personalities don't get heavily involved in "their books." But because I feel something special for this subject, I worked closely with the writers and editors. Until now, I had little appreciation of the amount of work that can go into a project like this, and I owe them my gratitude. I would like to thank Parton Keese, sports writer of The New York Times, for assembling the information and putting the initial ideas for the book on paper. I want to thank the editors and art directors of *Tennis* magazine, especially Stan Braverman and Laura Duggan, and books coordinator Charlene Cruson, for their assistance in so many ways. I'd like to pay tribute to the photographer, Mel DiGiacomo, who captured so well the sense of family and fun in his photos. And I'd like to thank Dick Kohfield for his fine instruction illustrations. Finally, I wish to express my appreciation to Cal Brown, the editor of the book, for his thoughtful suggestions and direction and for his work in revising the manuscript. Somehow all of these people managed to understand what tennis means to me, to my family and to yours.

John Newcombe
New Braunfels, Tex.
March, 1975

CONTENTS

INTRODUCTION

Someone once asked me: "John, you're either coming out of retirement or going back into it. One day you're winning Wimbledon or Forest Hills and the next you're giving it all up to go back with your family. Why is that?"

I guess the answer is "family." As much as I enjoy competing in tournaments and winning, I get a different, richer satisfaction when I'm with my wife Angie, my son Clint, and my little daughters, Tanya and Gigi. Although professional tennis has been a wonderful career for me and helped me in so many ways, I wouldn't want it to deprive me of watching Clint grow from a babe dragging a racquet bigger than he is around the court to a son who can rally with me. I'd hate not being there to hit the ball with the girls when they're starting out, and I wouldn't want to miss playing social tennis with Angie. I get a real kick out of playing with unprofessional players and on their own level.

To me, that's the joy of tennis. It's the only sport I know where you can play on any level and still have fun. It's one of the few competitive recreations I know where a family can participate together as long as they can swing a racquet. Family life has become too segmented during the last 15 years, not only in the United States, but all over the world. Most social activities are designed either for adults or for children, not both. Even adult activities are divided into those for men and those for women. And for children it's divided even more into sex and age groups.

I feel that the family that takes up tennis together is uniting with a common interest, as well as accomplishing something healthy and good for all of them.

That's the reason for this book. I've never really read anything especially aimed at how families can best enjoy tennis. I've never read any tennis instruction that was simple enough for any age, yet instructive for all. And while I have run across tennis books I've admired for their information and detail, they never seemed to put fun and relaxation ahead of cold textbook methods of winning. Few have tried to differentiate between the youngster just starting out and the man who has played for years, or the woman who plays once a week, or the man playing on his lunch hour. The family is probably the most important aspect of a person's life. How many tennis books relate to the husband playing with his wife, the mother with her son, and an older brother with a younger sister? I always wanted a book on tennis that was as much fun to read as tennis is fun to play. I always wanted a book that would show how to play tennis and enjoy doing it. And I always wanted a book that would not only improve my game, but also be so simple that every member of the family could understand it.

Some authors have been excellent in their studious analyses of tennis, but it might take a person five years to pick out a point he could use and identify with. It's the same on the court. So many people are over-taught and over-conscious of details, when playing tennis should actually be very simple. Every little detail on how to hit a forehand, say, isn't as important as finding out the basic element and then creating ways to enjoy learning it.

Families have been playing tennis together since the game was invented, so I don't think I've

discovered anything new. What I've tried to do in this book is add encouragement, with perhaps some new ideas based on my experience to make it easier and more enjoyable. You have to realize, first of all, that tennis is a game. As a game, it requires self-discipline and preparation to give the utmost enjoyment. So you have to be ready and willing to pay the small price it takes to get pleasure out of a game that offers more than enough for everybody.

The fact that a man can play with a man, a woman play with a woman, a woman with a child, or any combination of these and experience the maximum joy out of it, is what tennis is all about. When a person can not only hit the ball well, but control it too, it offers a challenge of competition and exercise that attracts the greatest fraternity of people I have ever known. People who play tennis are great people, and I think the game makes them great, not necessarily the other way around.

All right, we're all agreed that tennis should be fun. But how often does it happen, when a person starts out to learn to play, that tennis suddenly becomes as much a struggle as a game, with confusion over grips, what to do with your hips, wrists, legs, elbows or shoulders and how your feet should keep up with a ball that seems to bounce a dozen different ways? I don't believe tennis should be like that at all. To enjoy tennis, keep it simple without dwelling on complicated details.

As far as I'm concerned, there are only three basic functions involved in learning tennis: ball sense, movement and racquet control. And there are just three basic elements in every stroke: the preparation, the hitting zone and the finish.

Everything else falls into these categories, which I'll explain in Chapters 1 and 2. If I can just get you thinking about these few things instead of hundreds, I'll feel I've helped you get more fun out of tennis. Master these basics and the rest will fall in line. Free your mind from overwork.

Once you know the elements and basics, you'll be able to stop, analyze yourself and say: "Now this is what's happening. How do I overcome it?" Even if you are doing five or six things wrong, you should be able to identify the cause and adjust it. So, all of a sudden, by changing one thing instead of five or six, you can correct your stroke. You may slip back into your old ways after a while, but at least you will know the basic error you're making and adjust it without practice. Some teachers can discourage a person by trying to revamp an entire stroke. It's almost like starting out all over again with a different style. For an entire month, this person may not get a ball in the court, and tennis for him becomes a struggle and a bore. So he ends up quitting. That's not the proper approach at all.

I remember one guy who came to me and said, "Do you want to see my million dollar serve?"

"Million dollar serve?" I repeated with surprise.

"Yeah," he said, "I've had a lesson from nearly everybody in the world. I guess it's cost me about a million dollars. But you know, I still have a hitch."

"Let me see you serve," I told him. He did, and I looked at it and said, "You don't have a hitch."

He said, "What do you mean I don't have a hitch? I stop back here, don't I, while the ball is coming down?"

I said, "You don't have a hitch. You have a ball toss that's too high."

And sure enough, after he watched himself on a video replay, he adjusted his ball toss and eliminated the "hitch."

Changing a stroke or starting all over again is the worst thing a tennis player can do. You can destroy all the enthusiasm for tennis by doing that. Look for the key if the basics are there. No matter how weak a player may look, he can find some way to make the racquet meet the ball. You can't imagine the pleasure he'll get out of accomplishing just that simple thing. Nobody is so bad that he or she cannot enjoy tennis. In all my years of experience, I never found a person who couldn't play.

Sometimes the different levels of ability within the family can work to stunt a beginner's desire. The desire to help someone in your family learn tennis should go no further than just playing and enjoying. An advanced player shouldn't try to teach too much to a beginner. My six-year-old son Clint and I play sets now. I think that's the fastest way for a beginner to improve, and one which offers the highest motivation. I keep the ball in play, set balls up for him, and miss enough to keep the score close. Sometimes he wins, and sometimes I do, but we keep the ball in play a lot. That's the secret.

Over-instructing is a common fault, even among pros. The biggest help you can offer is to keep hitting balls to a learner. If he's got ball sense he'll pick up the rest. Every now and then you can whip in a comment such as, "Hey, your preparation's too slow" or "Toss the ball higher when you serve." You're letting him develop this way, instead of altering his game every time you play or practice together. If you see him holding his racquet like he would a frying pan, which is bad, I don't believe you should say, "That's the wrong grip." You're better off saying something like, "Hey, you'll be better off moving your hand around a little this way" or maybe "This is how Rod Laver holds his racquet." Family relationships should be strengthened through tennis, not strained.

There are always some beginners who lack natural ability. They're the ones who need a little more instruction, but not so much that they become frustrated. They need to rally a lot and develop their confidence. They need praise, rather than criticism. Parents who want so badly for their kids to play well that they start instructing them too harshly are making a bad mistake. Every time the child misses a ball, his father or mother tells him why he missed. It's one of the worst faults found in family situations.

Youngsters, being the way they are, don't always want to listen to their parents. Their parents are telling them things all day, anyway, and children don't feel like going out on the court and hearing more of it. So parents have to watch that they don't expect too much of their children, or of each other on the tennis court. The idea, remember, is to have fun.

Besides the joy of playing and improving one's game, tennis can breed the confidence one needs throughout life. I've always thought that beginners should be shown how to look like, act like and be players. I mean, you don't just go out on a court and start playing tennis. There's more to the game than hitting the ball. How you behave on court is as important as a proper stroke or being able to run. The earlier you start practicing the etiquette of tennis, the better off you'll be—as well as

everybody you'll come in contact with.

There are loads of ideas and tips here on the best way to practice, including games and drills to keep it fun, conditioning yourself properly, the kind of equipment you'll want (and won't want) as well as some rules of behavior which are basic to experienced players. Nothing can be more embarrassing, especially to beginners, than to realize too late that what they've been doing is not at all an acceptable way to act. Mental attitude is important, too. The worst kind of people to play with are the ones who, every time they miss, give a reason why they missed. It's just no fun playing with people like that. There's more to tennis than winning points.

Of course, I believe in tactics and strategy, too, but within the levels of play. Any champion can write how he serves a bullet, races to the net for the volley and slams it away for a winner. But can a mother identify with this high-powered way of playing? Or a man in an office who plays on his lunch hour twice a week? Most youngsters haven't achieved the strength or coordination they would need for such a game.

Obviously, there are shots for all levels of players, but I think the best way to learn these is to establish the foundations from which all styles develop. This makes a lot more sense to me than trying to teach everyone to play like Wimbledon champions the first time out.

Tennis can be simple, and fun, if you know what level of player you are. Armed with a few sound basics you can then progress as a player to a higher level. That's why this book is written the way it is. It begins with the basics and explains how you can use these basics to develop your game, in the most natural way for you. It's your development that is stressed, not specific twists or turns, so that you can improve in a way that lets you enjoy tennis.

Each chapter is illustrated with simple drawings to help you see each of the points we talk about. At the end of each chapter you will find a portfolio of photographs that show how Angie, Clint, Coach Mabry, some of the rest of our gang and I actually do the things we want you to do.

When you do reach a level that permits, there are refinements you can easily add to your game. Things like spin serves and two-handed backhands, lobbing against the wind, stop volleys and drop shots, using artificial lights or blazing sunshine to your advantage. There are lots of extra things that add dimensions to anybody's game. Try them. There are many ways to win and lose in tennis. Try them all, that's my motto.

I was lucky having parents who kept me interested in tennis when I was starting out. Now, I'd like to do the same for you. This book won't make you a Wimbledon champion, but it will give you a sound approach to learning and improving your tennis. You'll be able to spot yourself and members of your family. You'll be able to take simple elements and build your game from a sound base in the most natural way for you. Simplicity and enjoyment are the keys. I'm sold on it. Even if I weren't a professional myself, I'd want my children to learn tennis this way so they'd have the foundation on which to build a sound and happy game.

Believe it or not, even I learned something from this book while preparing it. It made me more aware of the importance of tennis to my own family. It also reminded me that I should not expect too much from Angie and the children, but instead that tennis affords me one opportunity to share something with them and have fun.

To us nothing is more fun than a social
game of tennis. It's relaxing to walk to
the courts in the country surroundings.
Our dog Pancho wholeheartedly agrees.
Playing tennis for exercise always
brings that kind of smile to Angie's face
—and mine, too.

*A bucket of balls, a tennis court and Mom
(that's me, grinning at left) and Dad make
Clint a very contented young boy (that's an
understatement). Tanya, our little daughter
in the picture below, is not gifted with
Clint's ball sense—she doesn't seem too sure
of our cameraman, either. Playing tennis
together as a family makes all of us happy.
I know John certainly can't relax like that
(below, right) with Connors or Laver.*

Clint actually taught himself to serve by watching others (left). At four he had an idea and at five he could serve quite well. In the picture below, Tony Roche (left) and Ron Ely (next to Tony) go in for some small talk between shots with Coach Mabry (at right) and me. Angie seems to want a breather. I guess it's obvious we think tennis is fun (far right).

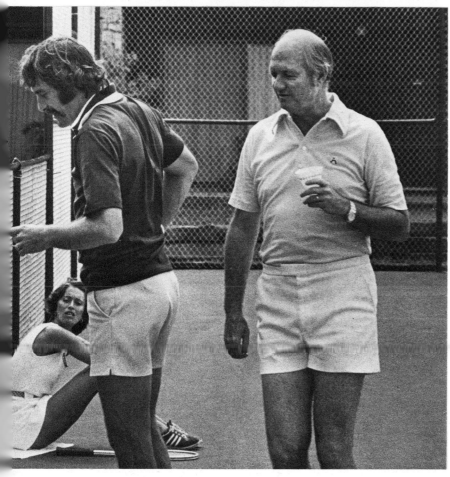

CHAPTER 1: A SIMPLE FOUNDATION

Tennis, to begin with the basics, is a game played with a racquet, a ball and a court (*see illustrations #1 and 2*). The idea is to knock the ball back and forth across the net. First you learn to get the racquet on the ball and then you learn to get the ball over the net. Once you learn those two things, you'll never forget them. It's like learning to walk. From that point on, learning how to improve becomes a simple process. All you have to know is what stage of development you've reached.

No one is a computer. If you feed too much information into a learning player's mind, he becomes confused and can't digest it. Worse, tennis is no longer fun, but a boring task. I don't want that to happen.

BASIC LEARNING CONCEPTS

There are three basic concepts to learn in tennis. The first is to see the ball coming toward you and judge where it will bounce. I call this *ball sense*. The second is to move yourself to the ball and still give yourself room to swing. I call this *movement*. The third is to develop control and feel of the strings of your racquet so you can hit the ball. This is called *racquet control*.

Everything in tennis is a refinement of these three basics whether you're a beginner, a weekend or a tournament player, whether you're a man, a woman or a youngster and whether you're left-handed, right-handed or ambidextrous. They are easy to learn by all members of the family. You can begin to play immediately with these three concepts and build your game around them. How quickly you advance depends on how well you can adapt to these concepts. The rest of this book will constantly refer back to ball sense, movement and racquet control.

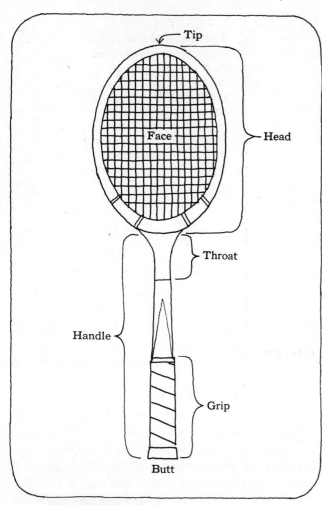

1. TENNIS RACQUET
This is a wooden racquet but they are also made of metal and fiber glass. Note the names of each part so you can refer to them easily.

BALL SENSE

Ball sense is knowing where the ball is going to bounce and having a vision of the line of flight it will take when it leaves your racquet or your opponent's racquet. Some people have more ball sense than others because they've been involved in other sports where bouncing, throwing, catching or hitting a ball has become part of their experience. A person without ball sense usually wants to run straight to the spot where the ball is landing instead of judging where its bounce will take it. All of a sudden, he finds himself too close to the ball and is forced to react awkwardly to hit the ball at all (*see illustration #3*).

To achieve ball sense, you must be able to identify the arc and bounce of the ball as it comes toward you. It's easier to see this bounce if you stand about two-and-a-half feet behind the baseline rather than in the middle of the court.

At first, I might tell a beginner to let the ball bounce without hitting it. Just watch the line of flight, or the path of the ball, to see what it does. Notice how high it is when it clears the net. Then watch how high it bounces. You want to get your racquet back on the same basic level as this bounce (*see illustration #4*).

This knowledge will tell you where to swing your racquet. You should take your racquet back at the height you think the ball will bounce. You should stroke forward level with the top of the ball's bounce. For example, if the ball comes over the net a little higher than your head, you can anticipate a high bounce around shoulder level

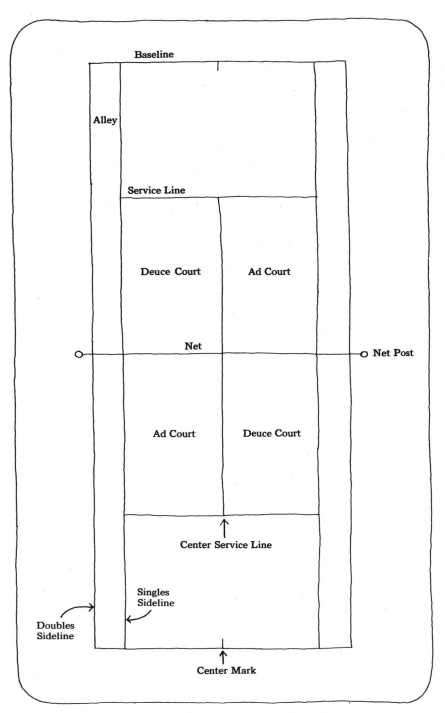

Baseline

Alley

Service Line

Deuce Court   Ad Court

Net   ○——○ Net Post

Ad Court   Deuce Court

Center Service Line

Singles
Sideline

Doubles
Sideline

Center Mark

2. TENNIS COURT

The lines and areas of a tennis court have names that are a mixture of common sense and tradition. The service courts are traditionally called "ad" and "deuce" in reference to the score a player can have when serving into those courts.

3. DON'T OVERRUN THE BALL

In developing ball sense, watch the height and direction of the ball as it comes over the net. You don't want to run to the spot where the ball bounces, but rather to the spot where the bounce will take it. That way you will have a chance to hit a well-coordinated shot, not the awkward one shown below.

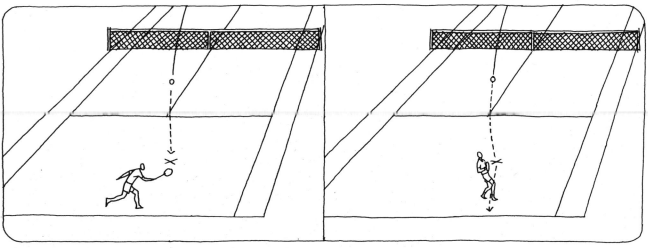

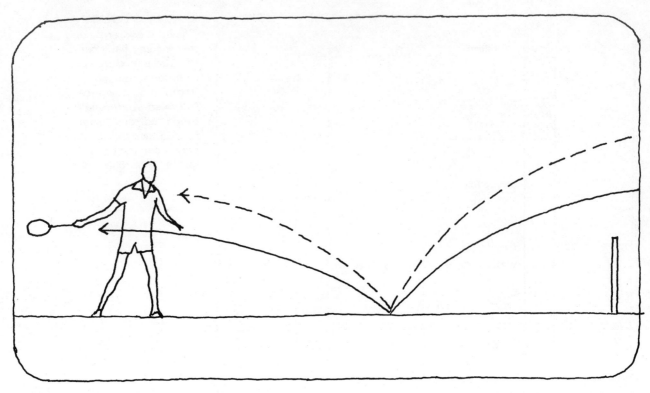

4. HEIGHT OF THE BOUNCE
Watch the line of flight of the ball. The higher it comes over the net, the higher it will bounce.

and prepare to swing your racquet at that height. Following the arc of the ball as it comes toward you will enable you to judge the height of the bounce and, thus, the line that your racquet should follow in preparing and stroking the return.

If the ball clears the net by about three feet, it should land in the back third of the court. It usually makes little difference what the speed is. If the ball clears the net by only five or six inches, you can expect it to land nearer the net (*see illustration #5*). This knowledge alone will help you gauge whether to retreat or to hold your position.

Here's something that will help you build better ball sense. Most balls, coming to your side of the court, will bounce inside an area shaped like a figure-eight (*see illustration #6*). In fact, about 80 per cent of the balls land in this area. You can virtually ignore balls that land outside this figure-eight—in the corners near the baseline or right by the net—and concentrate on getting the maximum number of balls back.

It's never too early to mention the importance of watching the ball. The best way, I think, is to watch the side of the ball closest to you and try not to let your eyes wander away from the line of flight. However, watching the ball can be overdone. In concentrating on the ball, don't forget to hit it. My son Clint is an example. I once told him to watch the ball as closely as he could, and he did just what I told him. He watched the ball come toward him, watched it bounce and watched it go right by him. The only thing was, he forgot to swing.

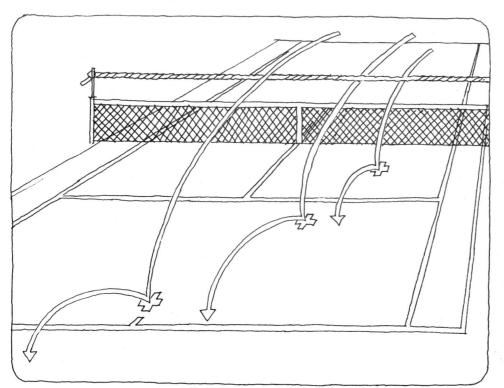

5. DEPTH OF THE BOUNCE

If a ball clears the net by about three feet (as indicated at left by the rope), it should land in the back third of the court, the backcourt. Balls that clear the net lower than the rope will land either in mid-court or close to the net.

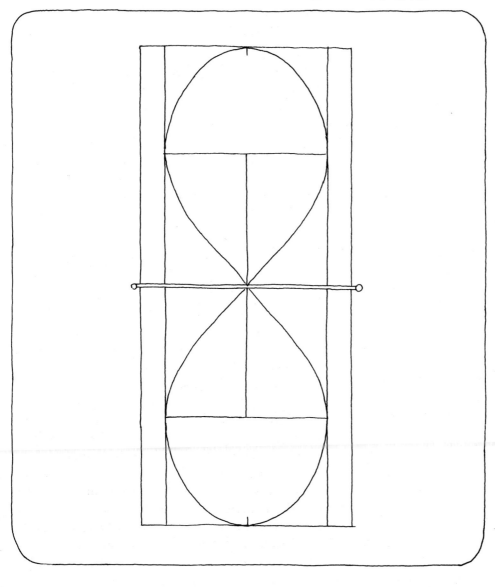

6. AREA OF THE BOUNCE

About 80 per cent of all balls will land within this figure-eight shaped area. Beginners will do well to concentrate on protecting this portion of their court from a position behind the baseline.

7. MOVING ON COURT

Getting to a ball or forcing your opponent to do so involves moving back and forth in three ways, two of which are emphasized here: side to side and forward and back. You will become aware of the third way, up and down, as you develop your ball sense and skill as a player.

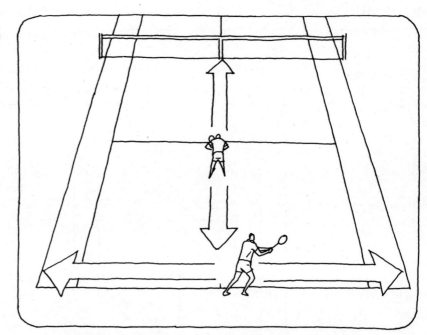

8. IMPROVE YOUR MOBILITY

To quicken your court coverage and improve your ability to move from side to side and forward and back, try this running-the-lines drill. Starting from the baseline, skip sideways to the sideline, run up to the service line, skip sideways to the other sideline and then run backwards to the baseline. Repeat several times.

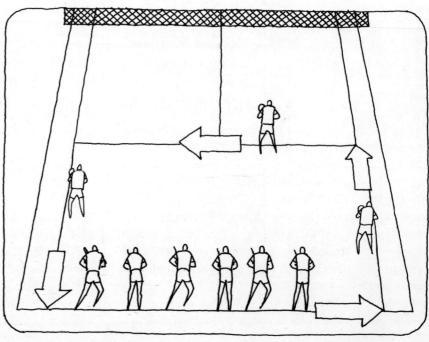

MOVEMENT

Movement refers to your ability to get to the place where you can retrieve the ball and, at the same time, allow yourself room to swing the racquet and hit the ball. Movement involves three dimensions: side to side, forward and back, and up and down (see *illustration #7*).

If you are playing with beginners, most balls will land around the service line. So, if you position yourself about two feet behind the baseline at the center of the court you will be able to judge where the shots are coming and where to move to get them. From this station you will have to move only one or two steps either forward or to the side to get the majority of balls hit to your side of the net. After each shot, you should always return to the baseline position at the center of the court so you'll be ready for the next shot.

At first, you will be most conscious of your movement from side to side, and forward and back. As your ball sense and ability to move increase, you will become more aware of and more able to handle balls bouncing at different heights. The whole objective, remember, is to get yourself to the ball in position to hit it. If a ball is coming straight at you, you will have to move away from the line of flight (either to the right or left) to give yourself room to swing the racquet into the ball. Normally, you will need between three and five feet between you and the ball to have room to swing your racquet into the ball. This distance will depend on your height and the length of your arms. To find out what distance you will need for a free swing, extend your racquet straight out in front of you and have a friend measure the distance from your shoulder to the tip of your racquet.

In moving to the ball, you will discover that you have to adjust your strides. You will sometimes have to take shorter, quicker steps, or sidesteps, or you may have to slide your feet. This is known as footwork. We have a little drill in our tennis clinics that helps in learning these quick, sliding sidesteps. It's called "running the lines," where pupils move quickly around the court following the baseline, sidelines and service line (see *illustration #8*). This is pretty gruelling sometimes, but it's a great way to learn the footwork you'll need for good movement.

Most beginners are one step short on footwork. By that I mean that they miss out on the final step into the ball. You must learn to approach the ball in such a way that the final step you take is forward in the direction you want to hit. That extra forward step will help you swing properly.

If you are a beginner I wouldn't want you to worry too much about footwork. I'll give you a little tip: if you concentrate on getting your racquet back, your footwork will work out, pretty much by itself.

Finally, all players, from beginner to advanced, should remember that an important part of movement is recovering; that is, returning to a balanced position after making the shot, ready for the next one.

RACQUET CONTROL

The third basic concept is racquet control, which means simply controlling your racquet head and developing a feel for the strings. This can begin as early as a youngster or beginner can pick up a racquet and bounce a ball up and down with it. First, you want to learn how to meet the ball squarely with the strings of your racquet. Squarely means with the racquet face parallel to the net, neither angled up nor down, nor to the side. When you can do this consistently, you'll find your body position will adjust almost instinctively and you will not get too close or too far from the ball.

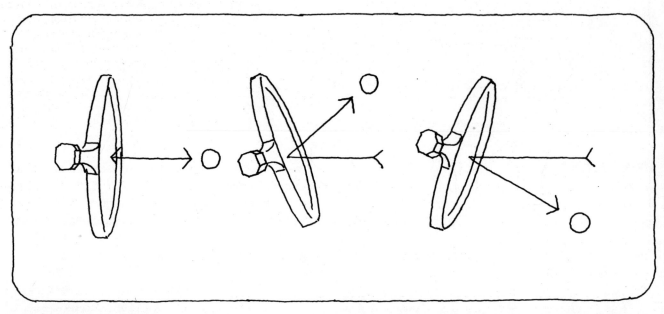

9. RACQUET ANGLES

The angle of your racquet determines the trajectory of the ball. If you contact the ball flat (left) you'll return it level; angle the racquet upward (center) and the ball will go up; angle the racquet down (right) and the ball will go down.

Racquet control is knowing where the face of the racquet is.

The basic function of racquet control is control of the strings themselves. The strings of the racquet are like a flat board. They determine both the direction and trajectory of the ball.

If you could see the ball leaving the racquet in slow motion, you'd see that when the strings are angled up, the ball goes up. When the strings are angled down, the ball goes down (*see illustration #9*). You would also see how the different angles of the racquet cause the ball to go in different directions.

Timing your swing

Another function of racquet control is moving the racquet in harmony with your body weight. In other words, as your racquet goes back, your weight should go back. When your racquet moves forward, your weight should move forward with it. This is known as timing.

Have you ever seen a grown man struggling to hit the ball, while on the next court a small girl is hitting the ball with smooth, powerful strokes? The man is struggling because his racquet is going north while his weight is going south. The girl has her weight and her racquet going north at the same time. The man's own strength and weight are fighting him instead of helping him to use his power

NO   YES

10. USE YOUR WEIGHT
Have your weight and your racquet move in the same direction for good timing and maximum power. A good stroke is the result of "putting your weight into the shot." If your weight is back and your racquet forward, you'll hit a weak, awkward shot like the one shown at left.

to advantage. She's getting the maximum out of her little stroke because her racquet and body weight are traveling in the same direction (*see illustration #10*).

When you play tennis, is your weight getting through before your racquet? Or your racquet before your weight? Don't step forward before you are ready to hit the shot. That will isolate your body from the shot and force you to use your hand and wrist to hit the ball. Or it would cause you to fall backward. Either is acceptable, of course, when you are in trouble. But, neither is desirable if you want to have consistent accuracy and power.

However, don't think so much about where your weight is that you forget to move the racquet through the ball. You want to feel the ball staying on your racquet a long time, not a short time, after you've made contact with it. As you hit, get the feeling that you ride right on through for maximum control and power. Your racquet and body weight must move forward together for correct timing.

When you have to chase a ball, you probably won't get a great deal of weight into the shot unless you get there early enough to take that final step in the direction you want to hit the ball. But if you can just get there to the best of your ability, and then swing the racquet through the ball, I think you'll find that your weight will come through naturally.

11. SHORTER RACQUETS

Children often hit more easily by starting to play tennis with a short-handled racquet (left), graduating to an intermediate (center), then a standard size handle (right) as their strength permits.

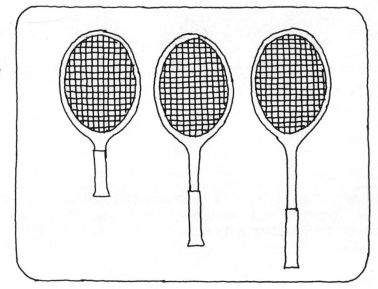

12. GRIPPING THE RACQUET

Learning to hold the racquet is easy if you place the palm of your hand on the racquet face and simply slide it down to the handle. Close your fingers around the handle and you'll have a proper forehand grip.

As a beginner, grip the racquet by the strings to get the feel of racquet control. The palm of your hand and the face of the racquet will be in the same direction. Little by little move your hand down the handle to retain the feeling of controlling your racquet.

How to gain awareness of strings

Learn to think of the racquet head as an extension of your arm and hand. The longer the racquet, the more difficult this becomes, of course. Since it is easier to hit the ball with a real hand than with a long extension of it, I sometimes recommend starting out children with shorter racquets. And small children should not only have a shorter racquet, but a lighter one, too. When Clint was a baby, he had a tennis racquet that was practically the face of a racquet and a handle, with no throat to speak of (*see illustration #11*).

When beginners first start holding their racquets, I usually have them put the palm of the hand on the face of the racquet. This gives an immediate awareness of the strings, and the relationship of the hand to the racquet face. I then tell them to slide their hand down the handle so they can see this relationship (*see illustration #12*).

One of the best ways to feel the palm of the hand and the racquet face working as a unit is to let a beginner start hitting the ball while his fingers are touching the strings (*see illustration #13*). From there he can work his hand down the racquet throat little by little until he comes to a proper grip at the handle. If he does this properly, he'll end up with a comfortable feeling as well as a good idea about racquet control.

In the final analysis, though, how often you handle the racquet—on and off the court—will determine how well your racquet control develops. The more you handle it, the more familiar you are going to become with the racquet. Pick it up and swing it every day, even if you can't get out to play. You'll be surprised how this helps. Familiarity breeds control.

14. COMFORTABLE GRIPS

This is how your grip will look for the forehand (left) and the backhand (right). The key to a comfortable grip is having to make only a minor change from forehand to backhand. The forehand is easily achieved by having the palm of your hand in the same plane—facing in the same direction—as the face of your racquet. For the backhand, rotate your hand slightly counter-clockwise from the forehand grip until it is comfortably on top of the grip.

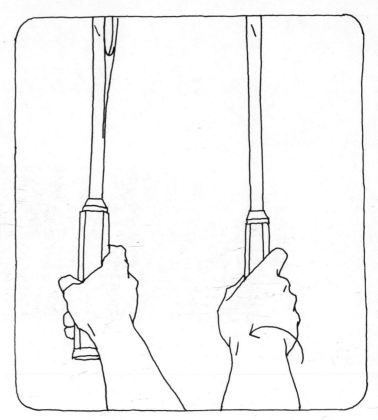

How to hold the racquet

This brings us quite naturally to the subject of grip. Frankly, I feel that how you hold the racquet is largely a personal matter which depends on your own anatomy—how big your hand is, the flexibility of your forearm and wrist, and how long your fingers are. Here is what you must know about your grip to make it work effectively. The grip is your only connection with the racquet. Therefore, you should hold the racquet in a way that encourages maximum racquet control.

The simplest way to achieve this is to have the palm of your hand on the same plane—that is, looking in the same direction—as the face of your racquet (refer back to *illustration #12*). This, of course, applies to the forehand. The grip will change slightly for the backhand. It will move more on top of the racquet handle with the palm facing more toward the ground. This slight change will allow you to swing as freely on the backhand as you do on the forehand. The reason is that when you swing, the natural rotation of your forearm is not the same on both sides of your body. This slight grip change will allow for this variation. I think the key to a good grip, though, is having to make only a minor change from forehand to backhand (*see illustration #14*).

You may want to spread your fingers on the grip. This gives you more comfort and control of the racquet. If you grip with the fingers tightly

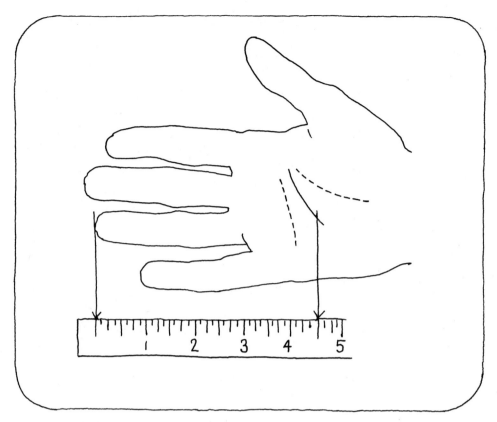

15. YOUR GRIP SIZE
You can determine your grip size by measuring the distance from the top of your fourth finger to the middle crease in the palm of your hand.

bunched together in what I call the hatchet grip, you will form an "L-shaped" angle between the arm and racquet which tends to separate the two. The idea is to feel the racquet and strings as an extension of your hand. Spreading your fingers puts the racquet more in the palm of your hand and gives you the feeling, on the forehand, of the palm and racquet face going in the same direction. On the backhand, it will put the racquet more in line with the arm and you'll have the sensation that the racquet is more an extension of your arm.

In choosing a racquet, you want to get one with the right size grip for your hand. Racquets are made with different sized grips for this purpose. You can pretty well figure out the correct size for your hand by measuring the length from the tip of your fourth, or ring finger, to the middle crease in the palm of your hand (*see illustration #15*). For most adults this will be between four and five inches; for children it may be less. Racquets are marked by manufacturers to indicate grip size with a small sticker on the side of the handle.

To sum up, then, the three basic concepts of tennis are ball sense, movement and racquet control. Ball sense tells you how and where the ball is coming at you. Movement gets you to that ball in a position to return the shot. Racquet control is your ability to direct the racquet so that you can hit the ball. Everything that follows in this book is based on these concepts, and refers back to them.

HOW TO ACQUIRE BALL SENSE

I encouraged Clint at an early age to get the feel of the ball. Tossing it up, dropping it in a can, throwing it, catching it, all helped him learn ball sense, even when he was too small to swing a racquet. (The pictures on this page were taken when Clint was 15 months old. He's six now.) It is very difficult for a father to teach his son, so I try to limit my verbal instruction to Clint. Encouragement is the main thing.

MOVEMENT ON THE COURT

The three basic movements in tennis are from side to side, forward and backward and up and down. I'm shown, above, moving to my right with a turn and crossover step. Notice the extension of my right arm, showing that I have allowed plenty of room to swing. Angie is showing good forward movement at right. Her body is side-on to the net, her racquet position excellent. This will enable Angie to stop and stroke the ball properly. My student Greg (left) bends his knees to get down to a low volley. This is one of the advanced movements in tennis, and he's showing good form.

LEARNING RACQUET CONTROL

Drills like this one Clint and I are doing improve racquet control for adults and children. Bouncing a ball up and down with the racquet helps to get the feel of the ball on the strings. Several thousand balls can be hit in a short time either on the court (left) or around the house. Dropping the ball and hitting it was the first stroke Clint learned (above). He'll practice this shot by himself. Later, he will be able to practice his forehand at mid-court, a good drill if the child is not strong enough to hit from the baseline, or rally with his dad in the service court (right).

FOREHAND AND BACKHAND GRIPS

The grip is your only connection with the racquet. The detail of how you grip is a personal matter, but for good racquet control you should follow two guidelines. First, on the forehand (which I'm demonstrating at left) keep the palm of the hand and the face of the racquet on the same plane, facing in the same direction. This will give you the feeling of the racquet face swinging with the palm of your hand. Second, the backhand (at right) requires a slight counterclockwise rotation of the hand. The reason for this rotation is so your racquet can swing freely on the backhand side rather than having to be pulled through unnaturally. Notice that the heel of my hand has moved but the palm has not moved due to the structure of my forearm. Yours may look a little different.

CHAPTER 2: THE BASIC STROKES

Now it's time to talk about how to hit the ball. There are only three kinds of strokes in tennis: 1) putting the ball in play, or a serve; 2) hitting the ball after it bounces, or a ground stroke; and 3) hitting the ball before it bounces, or a volley. It's that simple.

The easiest of these three types of strokes is putting the ball in play, because you are initiating the shot. You don't have to react to a ball hit by your opponent. All you do is lift the ball in the air and hit it with an overhand motion just as if you were throwing a ball. Once you can do this, you have learned the basic serve.

Hitting the ball after it bounces is harder than the serve because you have to see the oncoming ball and react to it. To hit a ground stroke, you need enough ball sense to know where and how high the ball will bounce. You also need to move in position to get your racquet on the ball close to the top of its bounce. And, your racquet must hit the ball so that it will go back across the net.

Hitting the ball before it bounces, or volleying, is both easier and harder than ground stroking. The volley is easier because you do not have to add speed to the ball. All you have to do is contact the ball with the racquet head, almost like catching the ball on the strings. The volley is harder than a ground stroke for beginners because it allows less time to react to the oncoming ball.

BASIC STROKE ELEMENTS

There are three and only three elements common to all of these strokes—the preparation, the hitting zone and the finish.

To hit a ball coming at you, you will need to bring the racquet back on one side of your body or

16. PREPARATION
The first element of stroke-making is the preparation—bringing your racquet back to one side of your body (side-on to the net), ready to come forward to hit the ball (above).

17. HITTING ZONE
The second element of the stroke involves swinging the racquet forward and contacting the ball in front of your body (below).

18. FINISH
The third element of the stroke is the follow-through, completing your stroke after the ball has been contacted by following the path of the ball with your racquet.

the other. That's what I mean by *preparation* (*see illustration #16*). Then you will swing the racquet forward and make contact with the ball. That's what I mean by the *hitting zone* (*see illustration #17*). Finally, your natural momentum will carry the racquet forward as if you were following the path of the ball. That's the *finish* (*see illustration #18*).

When you are ready to put the ball in play, you have to initiate the movement of the ball yourself. First, visualize the arc you will make with your racquet (*see illustration #19*) and then lift the ball into that arc (preparation). Then watch the ball as it is hit by the racquet (hitting zone), and finally follow through by letting the racquet complete the arc (finish).

The preparation, the hitting zone and the finish make up the swing for all strokes in tennis. **Let's** examine these elements more closely for the **three** basic kinds of strokes.

PUTTING THE BALL INTO PLAY

The serve, or putting the ball in play, is the only time in tennis that you have complete control of the ball. So, it makes sense to practice your serve to take advantage of this situation. You'll have plenty of time to prepare for your serve. Take your time. The better your preparation, the more accurate your serve will be.

You prepare by taking a comfortable stance a few inches behind the baseline. Your feet should be about shoulder width apart and placed so that a line drawn across your toes would point into the

service box you wish to hit. Hold the racquet and the ball in front of you with the racquet head pointing in the direction that you're going to serve. Now lift the ball into the air and hit with an overhand, throwing motion.

To hit the ball, bring your racquet up and place the strings on the ball with your arm and your body at full stretch. If your serves goes into the net, you simply move the toss a little farther back and the ball should clear the net easily. If the ball goes too far, move your toss forward. Don't worry if, at first, your serves go too deep. You can't play a ball that goes into the net but one that clears the net at least has a chance of starting the point.

Continue your motion as you hit the ball. Let your racquet follow the line of flight of the ball out into the court. Finish your serve by swinging the racquet across your body.

To put the ball into play with your serve, remember these three points: take time to prepare; visualize the arc of the hitting zone so that you can lift the ball into it; and finish with a full follow-through in the direction that the ball is going.

Now that you've learned how to put the ball into play, let's take a look at keeping the ball in play by hitting it after it bounces in your court.

HITTING THE BALL AFTER IT BOUNCES

For the forehand and backhand ground strokes, just relax and be ready to move to either side. In the best ready position you simply hold your racquet out in front of your body, the throat

19. PUTTING THE BALL IN PLAY

For the serve, the basic elements are preparation—(1) visualizing the arc that your racquet will make and (2) lifting the ball into that arc; the hitting zone—(3) watching the racquet strings contact the ball; and the finish—(4) following through by letting the racquet complete the arc.

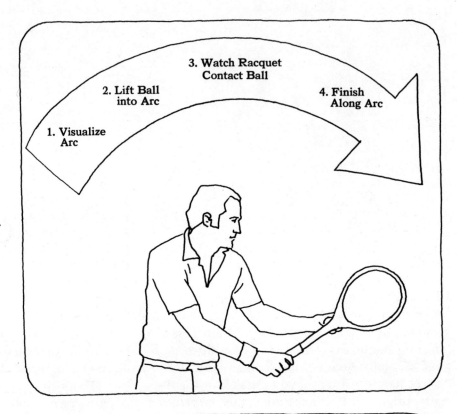

1. Visualize Arc

2. Lift Ball into Arc

3. Watch Racquet Contact Ball

4. Finish Along Arc

20. READY POSITION

When you are waiting to hit a ground stroke, you should be in a good ready position with your racquet held out in front of you, supported by your free hand. Your body should be relaxed and ready to move to one side or the other to hit the ball.

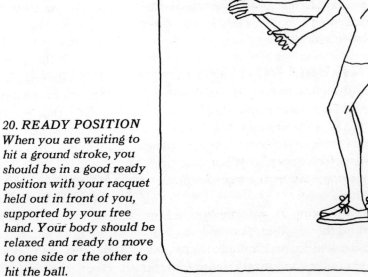

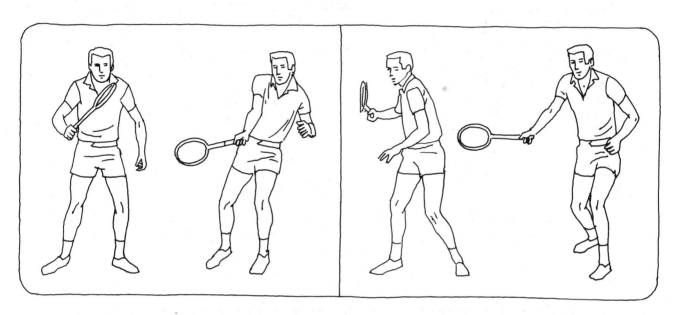

supported by the fingers of your free hand. Your knees are flexed and your body poised, ready to move in either direction before the ball bounces (see *illustration #20*).

From the ready position, you prepare for a forehand or a backhand by turning your shoulders to the right or left. This starts the backswing. Your racquet moves back with your body motion until the side of your body is to the net, a position we call getting "side-on" to the net. This gets your racquet back into a position to hit the ball (see *illustration #21*). The backswing is nothing more than drawing the racquet back with your hands and arms, at the same time allowing your body weight to follow the direction the racquet is moving.

Ground stroke preparation is very similar to walking up to the batter's box in baseball and getting ready to hit. You can tell if a hitter is comfortable, usually, even before the pitch is made. In the same way I can tell a player is in a comfortable position if his racquet head is back and ready to hit the ball.

There are several ways to bring the racquet back: you can loop it back or bring it straight back. What's important is that you hit the ball squarely from directly behind it and swing through along the

21. PREPARE EARLY
As soon as you sense the direction of your opponent's shot, get your racquet back by turning your shoulders so you are side-on to the net (right). If your movement is late, you'll rush your swing and hit too close to your body (left).

22. THE LINE OF FLIGHT
For an effective return shot, hit squarely from behind and follow through along the desired line of flight.

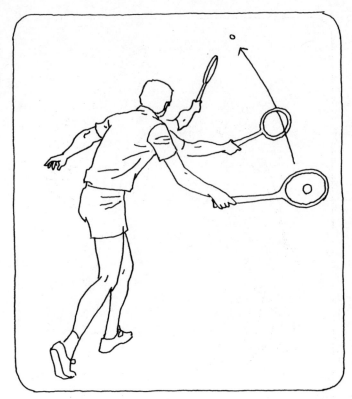

desired line of flight (*see illustration #22*).

When do you bring the racquet back? I like to draw a mental picture of a long bar or rod connecting my racquet head and my opponent's racquet head (*see illustration #23*). When my opponent's racquet head comes forward, it pushes my racquet head back into the ready position. As I drive my racquet head into the ball, it drives his racquet head back.

The forehand backswing is longer than for the backhand. For the forehand, you must get the racquet back early enough to have time to turn your body, get into position and be comfortable. A shorter and more compact backswing is better for the backhand because the shoulder on your hitting arm is in front of your body instead of behind it, as in the forehand. The backswing should go back far enough that you feel your hitting hand close to your back hip.

Your preparation should be smooth, not rushed. Some coaches cause pupils to rush their swings by yelling, "Get your racquet head back! Get it back!" A person who has too fast a swing usually prepares late and has to move his racquet back and forward

in the same motion. It should accelerate only as it comes forward to meet the ball to overcome the speed of the oncoming ball. You and your opponent may be competing with each other, but you're also in timing together. He hits his shot, you prepare. You hit yours, he prepares. You'll find there are rallies that have a definite sound of rhythm. You can almost play the game by ear—the ball hitting the ground, then your strings, then the ground on the opposite side, then your opponent's strings, and so on.

The hitting zone must be in front of you, that is, slightly closer to the net than your forward foot. While this is certainly important for the forehand, it's absolutely essential for the backhand. If you are right-handed, this means your right foot (*see illustration #24*). Any time contact gets behind that foot, you'll begin to hit the ball with the small muscle in your wrist instead of the big shoulder muscle. This is a major cause of tennis elbow.

The forward swing will cover roughly 180 degrees from backswing to follow-through. Think of a clock's hands moving from 6 o'clock to 12 o'clock. Anything beyond those limits is wasted, while

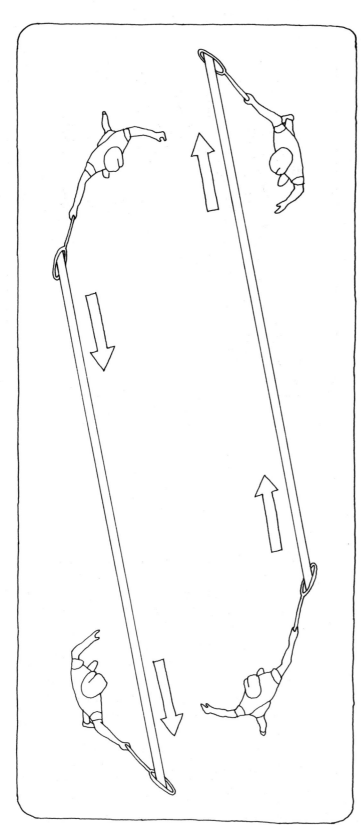

24. CONTACT POINT
It is important for good control of the stroke—and for preventing tennis elbow—to contact the ball while it is in front of your body. This is particularly essential for the backhand.

23. TIME YOUR PREPARATION
To get a better feel of when to bring your racquet back, imagine that your racquet and your opponent's are connected by a rod that alternately pushes his racquet back as you swing into the ball. This creates a rhythm to the motion. He hits, you prepare. You hit, he prepares, and so on.

25. "THROW" YOUR FOREHAND

Hitting a forehand ground stroke is like throwing a bucket of water on the ball. With your hitting hand on the bottom of the bucket, toss the water on the ball and follow through with a throwing motion along the path of the ball.

anything not reaching those points is short of full power.

I like to envision the forward movement of the forehand stroke as throwing a bucket of water on the ball. With your hitting hand on the bottom of the bucket, you toss the water on the ball, following through with a natural throwing motion along the flight of the ball (*see illustration #25*).

The forward movement of the backhand stroke is like drawing a sword up and out of its sheath. This is not a pulling action but one where the racquet is swept out and up (*see illustration #26*).

Make certain that you bring the racquet head into the ball along its line of flight. If you hit the ball at waist level, your stroke will have maximum leverage. If the ball arrives below waist level, then simply bend your knees and hit through the ball as if it were still waist high. If it's a high ball get your racquet up behind the ball's line of flight and finish high.

The finish is a very simple part of the stroke because it is a result of good preparation and swing. The finish is merely the completion of your stroke after the ball has been struck. Some people refer to this as the follow-through.

For a proper finish on ground strokes, allow the racquet head to continue forward along its swing path so that the tip of the racquet points to the fence on the opposite court. Your racquet should finish above your shoulder and above the top of the net as you view it (*see illustration #27*).

26. UNSHEATH YOUR BACKHAND

Hitting a backhand is like drawing a sword up and out of its sheath. This image will help you get in the correct position during your preparation—with your hand on your hip— and also help you envision the proper finish above your shoulder.

27. BACKHAND FINISH

To complete your backhand stroke, continue forward along the intended line of flight of the ball. Finish with your racquet above your shoulder, pointing at the fence on the opposite court.

28. VOLLEY PREPARATION

To prepare for a volley, you should feel as though you are crouched to sit on a high stool, with your knees bent and the racquet head held upright. Remember that there's little backswing on this shot. Try to hit the ball dead center on the strings.

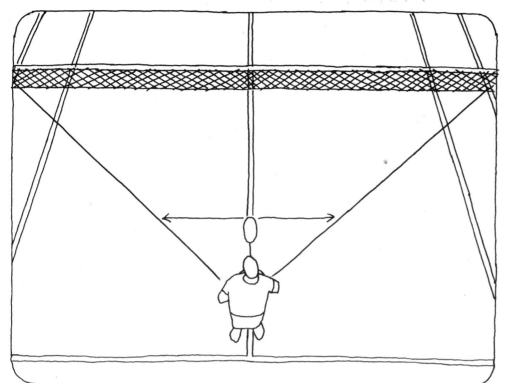

29. COVERING THE NET
Imagine a funnel with yourself as the base. You should be able to cover volleys anywhere within this funnel area by holding the racquet upright and working in a "V" in front of you. Your racquet hand should stay within the funnel for the best approach to the ball. Moving within this funnel will also give you the best angle to cut off the oncoming ball's line of flight.

HITTING THE BALL IN THE AIR

A ball that you hit in the air before it bounces (a volley) must be hit sooner and more firmly than a ground stroke, especially when you are close to the net. Therefore, the preparation must be quicker and shorter; the finish will also be shorter. In addition, the leverage of your racquet is different. You don't need a big backswing because the power of the ball coming at you has not been dissipated by bouncing on the ground. To handle this power keep the racquet head in a more upright position. This upright position lets you move the racquet to the ball faster and earlier. If you bend at the knees and keep your racquet head higher, you'll have more shoulder-high volleys to hit. You should almost feel as though you are poised to sit on a high stool (see *illustration #28*). This is the ideal position of leverage for hitting volleys.

The most important objective in volleying is to be sure that the ball hits the strings of your racquet dead center.

You usually don't have time for a backswing when you're at the net, so you should practice a volley without it. Imagine you're standing at the base of a funnel in your net position. The funnel extends from the two net posts and converges on you (see *illustration #29*). Your racquet should stay in front of your body inside these imaginary sides of the funnel. Your racquet head should be upright and work in a "V" in front of you so as you move forward on a shot, you can cut off the oncoming ball's line of flight.

I've told you all you need to know about hitting the ball across the net, which is what tennis is all about. If you can put the ball in play, hit the ball on a bounce and hit the ball in the air, you're ready to play tennis. Improving on these basics means perfecting your ball sense, movement and racquet control. This will lead to more consistency, and more fun on the court.

Even if you are an advanced player, you will be able to improve if you follow the basic simplicity of the game outlined in this chapter. Even complicated, advanced situations can be simplified if you think of the basics—putting the ball in play, getting the right movement or making sure of your preparation for each shot. For example, a return of serve is nothing more than hitting the ball on one bounce. If you think of it in terms of ball sense, movement and racquet control you will return a lot more serves.

If you can get the ball back and forth across the net using these principles, you are ready to enjoy the game. You have the proper foundation to go on to more advanced stages of tennis.

BASIC WAYS TO HIT:
VOLLEY, GROUND STROKE, SERVE

There are only three kinds of strokes in tennis—a ball that is hit before it bounces (the volley), which John is illustrating below left, a ball that is hit after it bounces (a ground stroke) as I am doing below, and a ball that you put into play (the serve), which Clint is doing at far right. The upright position of John's racquet is slightly exaggerated, but indicates an important point for the volley, which is to keep the racquet head above the wrist.

THE BALL TOSS

Here John is showing Clint the ball toss, which is simply lifting the ball above you, into the arc your racquet will swing on. Clint's basic serve is nothing more than an overhand motion, almost like throwing a ball.

STROKE ELEMENTS:
PREPARATION, HITTING ZONE, FINISH

Every tennis stroke is easy to learn if you think of it as just preparation, hitting zone and finish. Even at the age of six, Clint has no trouble with this concept. Here he has prepared well (left) by turning his body side-on to the net and has swung both the racquet and his weight back in the same direction. However, I would like to have seen him cradle the racquet in his left hand on the backswing. His hitting zone (center) is well in front of his leading foot, and he is swinging level along the flight of the ball. The only criticism I could make here is that his racquet face is a little open at impact. At the finish (right), his racquet is pointing to the fence on the other side of the court.

THE BACKHAND GROUND STROKE

Angie's backhand (at left) indicates good preparation with her racquet back early and her weight moving with the racquet. The hitting zone is well in front of her body, an important point in the backhand. Her weight has moved forward so that she can lean into the shot. Angie's finish is good, with the racquet above shoulder height, pointing in the direction of the ball's flight. Angie has a beautiful backhand stroke. Her body weight and shoulder and arm positioning are just about perfect.

THE FOREHAND GROUND STROKE

My forehand (below) is one of the best. Several things stand out here—a simple preparation (frames 1-4), meeting the ball in front of the body (frame 6) and a good follow-through (frames 8 and 9). Notice that I start from a good ready position (frame 1). My weight is equally balanced on both feet, the racquet cradled easily in front of me. In this position I can turn left or right to hit either a forehand or a backhand. On a forehand, the most important thing is to turn and you'll notice the steps that I take to get my racquet back. My shoulders move around, put me side-on to the net and help get my racquet back (frames 2-4). As the ball bounces toward me, I move forward into the hitting zone (frames 5-7). This gives me the correct timing to make contact just as my weight moves forward. Pay close attention to my eyes, which stay on the ball until it has left the racquet; this helps to coordinate my body weight with the stroke. I try to hold the ball on the racquet as long as possible. You'll notice that my finish is high. I start from a low position and swing up and through the ball, which puts a slight amount of roll or topspin on my shot.

CHAPTER 3: PLAYING THE GAME

If you can hit the ball over the net and into the opposite court, you're ready to enjoy tennis—by playing it. To play tennis, you must learn to contend with an opponent and to keep your shots within the boundaries of the court.

In the beginning, you simply hit the ball back and forth with little control of its direction or distance, hoping the other guy will miss. You are just trying to keep the ball in play, and mostly from the back of the court since you do not have the experience to produce shots from mid-court or at the net.

A beginner can put the ball in play with his serve, return most other beginners' serves and hit the ball in the air when he has to. None of these shots are meant to be winners necessarily. The more balls you get back, the more points you will win as a beginner. The majority of points are won on errors (or lost on errors if you're a pessimist).

A beginner quickly learns that his best shot from the baseline is a ball hit deep to his opponent's baseline. The more often you can hit shots to that depth, the better off you will be. Of course, you make mistakes, too, and so does your opponent. If you hit short, it makes him come in. If your ball goes to his backhand, he may hit a weaker return. If you serve deep, you seem to be better off, too. If only you could hit to his backhand all the time. If only you could hit to his forehand when he is way over on the other side of the court. If only you could take advantage of his short return. If only you could volley better when at the net. If only you could get to the net to volley. If only you could hit over your opponent's head when he comes to the net.

You begin to realize that there is more to tennis

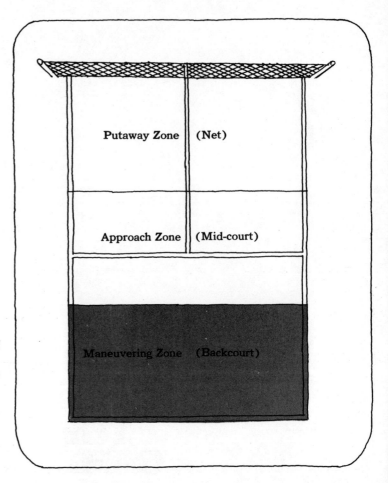

30. ZONES OF THE COURT
Think of the court as being divided into three zones—the maneuvering zone or backcourt, where you hit ground strokes and move your opponent around; the approach zone or mid-court area which you move through as you go to the net; and the putaway zone or net area, where you can win a point by putting the ball away.

than keeping the ball in play, more than just waiting for errors by your opponent. It begins to dawn on you that you can help bring about his mistakes. That's when you start on your way to becoming an intermediate player. It's not a sudden advancement, though.

WHAT CLASS PLAYER ARE YOU?

Tennis players can be divided broadly into three classes—beginners, intermediates and advanced. A beginner, as I have just indicated, is one who can put the ball in play and hit the ball over the net.

Your advancement as a player will come as a natural need to hit the ball from different positions on the court and to return shots in the direction and at the distance you want. I measure an intermediate or advanced player by his ability to control both the direction and the distance of his shots. I will explain this in a moment.

First, it will help you identify yourself as a player if you consider that the tennis court is divided into three zones. Your ability to play these zones will define your level as a player.

The first zone is the backcourt. I like to call this the *maneuvering zone*. This zone extends from the baseline to about six feet behind the service line, and covers the full width of the court (*see illustration*

#30). In this zone you can maneuver the ball and your opponent most easily and establish a position that gives you winning chances. The second zone is the middle of the court, an area I refer to as the *approach zone* because you must move through this zone as you approach the net. This zone extends about six feet on either side of the service line. This is the most difficult zone of the court to play from, requiring a high level of ball sense, movement and racquet control. The reason is that most balls will bounce somewhere in this zone. So, to return shots from the approach zone you must have keen reactions and very good control of distance and direction.

The third zone is the forecourt, which I call the *putaway zone*. This is the zone closest to the net. The main reason you go to the net is to put the ball away and win the point. Almost every shot played in this zone will be hit in the air before the ball bounces. The most important things to do in hitting a ball from the putaway zone are to have a firm grip and make sure the ball hits the center of the racquet, especially if you want to return the ball deep to your opponent's side.

An intermediate is one who has learned to control the direction and distance of his shots to such an extent that he can return shots from any of the

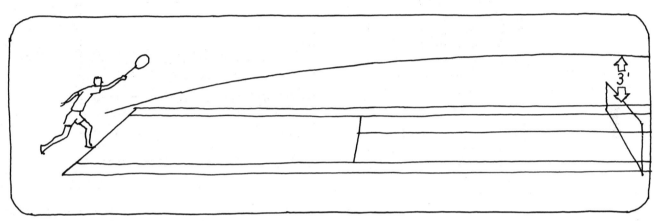

31. HIT SAFELY OVER THE NET
Never make a net error from behind the baseline. Hit the ball high over the net, about three feet, to make sure that it lands deep in your opponent's court.

three zones on his side of the net to the deepest zone of his opponent. In other words, he can retrieve a shot from his maneuvering zone, his approach zone or his putaway zone and return it in a desired direction to his opponent's maneuvering zone.

An advanced player has an even greater command of direction and distance. Not only can he return shots *from* any of the three zones on his side of the net, he can hit them *to* any zone he selects on the other side of the net.

A beginner should grow familiar with the backcourt in perfecting his ground strokes. The most important thing to remember in playing from the maneuvering zone is never to make a net error. Always hit the ball over the net, at least three feet above it (*see illustration #31*). This will ensure that it lands deep in the opposite court.

This is your first important step in learning to control the distance you hit the ball. You can't hit it out of court or into the net. To ensure that you don't make a net error from the maneuvering zone, take a full backswing, hit up and through the ball, and complete your follow-through. From the approach zone, your backswing is shorter, your swing more level, which causes the ball to clear the net by about two feet. From the putaway zone, your backswing is very short, sometimes no

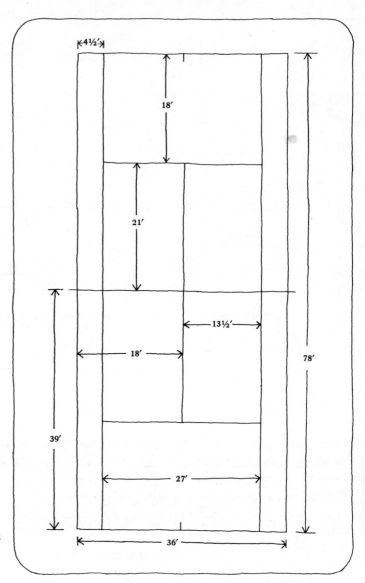

32. SIZING UP THE COURT
Keep the dimensions of the court in mind when you hit the ball. From backcourt to backcourt your ball will travel 70 to 80 feet but from mid-court to mid-court the distance may be 50 feet or less.

backswing at all. The main objective is placing the strings firmly on the ball in front of your body, so that the ball goes straight back over the net. From the maneuvering zone the ball will travel between 70 to 80 feet to your opponent's maneuvering zone; from mid-court to mid-court the distance is about 50 to 60 feet (*see illustration #32 for the actual dimensions of the court*). As you practice you will learn how much backswing and height are needed to produce the necessary distance.

CONTROLLING DIRECTION

The next step is learning how to hit the ball in the direction you want. You do this by changing the angle, or direction, of your racquet face. It may help to visualize this if you think of your racquet face wearing glasses. To hit the ball crosscourt these glasses, and thus your racquet face, would be looking diagonally across the court. To hit down the line, these glasses would be looking straight at the net so that your racquet strings are parallel to the net (*see illustration #33*). You'll find that it will

be easier to control the racquet's direction if you step forward with your front foot in the direction you want to hit. A checkpoint here is that a line across your toes would parallel your intended line of flight.

Improvement is not only a matter of talent. People who are restricted in talent can still move ahead in their development. It is actually easier for a beginner or intermediate player to show improvement than an advanced player. You might be able to improve your game as much as 40 per cent if you can refine your movement or the direction of your shots to the limit of your ability. Compare this with the top player who can only improve his game two or three per cent.

Do you ever say to yourself, "I'll never beat the guy I play each weekend?" You won't have to say that once you know what steps are needed to advance. If you are a beginner, just learning to hit the ball from side to side can alter the entire dimension of the game your opponent is used to seeing. In other words, if you can hit one shot

64

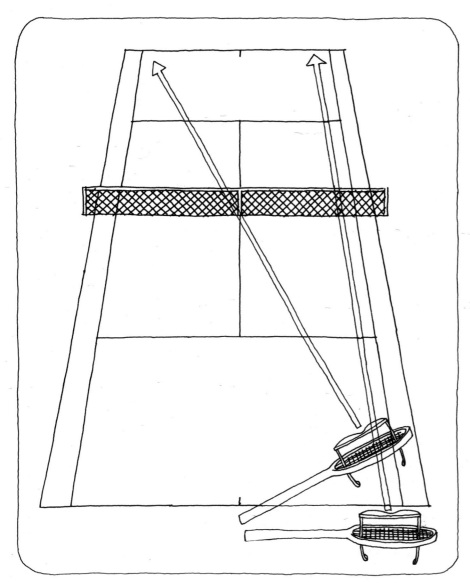

crosscourt, the next down the line and the next crosscourt, your opponent will have a whole new ball game to deal with. Furthermore, moving the ball side to side is much easier to learn than moving the ball forward and back.

If you are an intermediate player, you can develop your game dramatically through a better knowledge of the three zones of the court and how to play from them. By controlling the direction of your shots you can expose your opponent's weakness, discovering which is weaker, his backhand or forehand. By hitting a wide crosscourt shot to his forehand, for example, you set up a probable winning shot to his backhand weakness.

If you are an advanced player, you can improve by putting together combinations of shots that move your opponent through the three zones of his court and from side to side. This will expose his weakness in moving forward and back, which will test his ability to handle himself in all three zones.

Here, for example, is a drill we use to learn to hit from zone to zone. We call it the four-ball drill. It works like this. First, hit a crosscourt forehand from your maneuvering zone, then a deep backhand crosscourt from the same zone, followed by a forehand approach shot down the line, and finally winding up with a forehand crosscourt volley from your putaway zone. This takes you through each of the three zones and gets you accustomed to hitting the shots in sequence. In practicing this drill, make sure your practice partner has enough balls to keep feeding them to you in case you miss one of the shots in this sequence. Obviously, you can duplicate this four-ball drill in actual play. You can also change the order of this drill, so that you begin and end with backhand shots.

Your success and progress will ultimately depend on the foundation you have established at the very beginning. All top players have to return to the basics from time to time. For example, sometimes I find myself making errors on return of serve. Usually it's because I'm trying to force the ball into an area I shouldn't. That's when I decide to go back to a basic concept, which is simply returning the ball over the net so I keep it in play. That's the first object of the game, but at that point my needs and goals are exactly the same as the beginner and the intermediate.

The control of distance and direction will govern the development of your serve, just as they do in the ground strokes and volleys. A beginner simply puts the ball in play, with just enough idea of distance and the general direction to get the ball into the service court on the other side of the net. The intermediate player can place the serve in a specific direction. In other words, he can control the direction of his serve well enough to hit to his opponent's forehand, his backhand or straight at him. An advanced player adds depth, so that he has the ability to control both distance and direction in his serves. He can also add spin to the ball, a refinement I'll discuss in Chapter 4.

Learning to serve is something like learning to pitch in baseball. First, the pitcher learns to throw the ball over the plate, then he learns to move the ball around the plate and finally he acquires the skill to vary both the depth and the spin of his pitches. This is the same sort of development you need in tennis to advance from one level to the next.

KEEPING SCORE

The scoring in a tennis match is based more on tradition than everyday mathematics, but it's easy to master. Here are four main terms you should become familiar with: point, game, set and match.

How do you win a point? There are several ways and you should consult the rule book when you have any specific questions. Generally, however, a player wins a point if his opponent: 1) hits the ball into the net; 2) hits the ball after it has bounced twice; 3) returns the ball out of bounds (a ball is "good" even if it hits the baseline or sideline because the lines are actually considered part of the court), and 4) as happens less often, volleys the ball back before it has crossed to his side of the net. In serving, the receiver wins the point if the server "double faults," fails to put the ball in play in two attempts.

The first point a player wins gives him a score of 15, the second point—30, and the third point—40. If he wins the fourth point, he wins the game. If a player wins no points his score is "love," or zero. (The server's score always is given first). If both players have three points, that is, a score of 40-40, they are tied and the score is "deuce." To win the game now, one player must win two more points, not one. The first point after deuce is called "advantage." If the server wins it, the score becomes "ad-in;" if the receiver wins it, the score is "ad-out." If the player with the advantage wins the following point, he wins the game. However, if he loses that second point, he loses the advantage, and the score reverts to deuce. The game continues until the player with the advantage also wins the next point and the game.

The first player to win six games wins the set— unless the score is tied at five games each. Then, similar to the deuce situation in a game, they must keep playing until one player is ahead by two games (7-5 or 8-6, for example).

The match is won when one player wins two of three sets. The exception is some major men's tournaments where it's three of five sets.

PACE

Before we go to the next chapter, I want to say a word about pace, or speed.

As you advance from one level to the next you will become increasingly aware of the pace of the game. Pace refers to the speed of the ball. As you learn to hit squarely and with good timing, the speed of your shots will increase.

Pace is not just a matter of hitting harder. It is the capability of hitting slow, medium and fast. The speed of your medium-paced shots, that is the shots you can easily control, will increase naturally as your ability grows. All this really means is that your ball sense, movement and racquet control have progressed to the point that allows you to play with control at a greater pace. Pace, then, is the inevitable result of your development as a player.

In summing up, then, to progress, you must first know where you are in your tennis development. I think you can find yourself somewhere in this chapter. I have defined beginners, intermediate and advanced players in terms of how well they can control the distance and direction of their shots, and also in terms of their ability to play the different zones of the court—the maneuvering zone, the approach zone and the putaway zone.

I hope this gives you some specific goals to shoot for in improving your game. Let this be a kind of roadmap that guides you through your development. The whole purpose of this chapter has been to explain *what* you need to do to improve your game. In the next chapter, I will tell you *how to play* the shots you need to achieve this goal.

HOW TO CONTROL DIRECTION

The direction of your shots is controlled by the racquet face. Coach Mabry (right) is illustrating that the ball will go in the direction the strings are facing because the ball bounces off the racquet at right angles. When the racquet face is looking diagonally across the court, the ball will go crosscourt. When the racquet face is looking squarely at the net, with the strings parallel to the net, the ball will go down the line. These are the two basic directions for the intermediate player. It is easier to control the racquet's direction if you step forward with your front foot in the direction you want to hit, as I am doing in the picture below.

DIRECTING YOUR SERVE

A good drill for learning the direction of your serve is to stand at the baseline, as I am doing at right, in serving position and throw a ball into the opposite service court. This will help you develop the feeling of the motion you will need to hit your serves in the right direction.

THREE ZONES OF THE COURT

You can measure yourself as a player by how well you play in the three zones of the tennis court. In the putaway zone near the net (above), the most important thing is to meet the ball with the center of your racquet. John will be pleased that my racquet is properly upright here. In the approach zone, the middle section of the court (center), your main objective should be to keep your backswing shorter and swing level as John is doing. From the maneuvering zone in the backcourt, the one thing you don't want to do is hit the ball into the net. This isn't hard if you just think about finishing your stroke up and through like I'm doing (above, far right). Always try to clear the net by at least three feet, as John is demonstrating (below, far right).

CHAPTER 4: REFINEMENTS

The development of your tennis game requires that you continuously refine the basic strokes described in Chapter 2. As your experience increases and your confidence grows, you'll discover that there are many different ways to hit similar shots. The player who has the greatest selection of shots at his command will have the advantage over his opponents.

In refining your game, don't get bogged down with the details of the different strokes. You should first understand how an improved stroke will apply to your actual game. The mechanics of the stroke will follow naturally when you are ready. Thus this chapter will be concerned as much with helping you understand how the refinements fit in your game as with the details of the improved strokes.

The refinements I'm going to suggest are not just for advanced players. They are improvements you must learn if you want to change the level of your game. Of course, there are even more sophisticated refinements to carry you to yet a higher level. You can never know enough about tennis.

THE MANEUVERING ZONE
Ground strokes

When you play from the backcourt or maneuvering zone, you rely on ground strokes to move your opponents around and maintain your control of the game. Remember, the ball need not move faster than your opponent can run. Just stroke the ball steadily and you'll find that your shots will pick up "pace." That is, the ball will penetrate your opponent's court rather than sit up weakly.

Maneuvering an opponent from the backcourt is quite simple. Your object is to make as few errors as possible and force your opponent either to hit

34. MOVE YOUR OPPONENT

To be able to control the game, you must know how to move your opponent around the court and keep him off balance. The three directions you can move him by employing different kinds of shots are side to side, forward and back, and up and down.

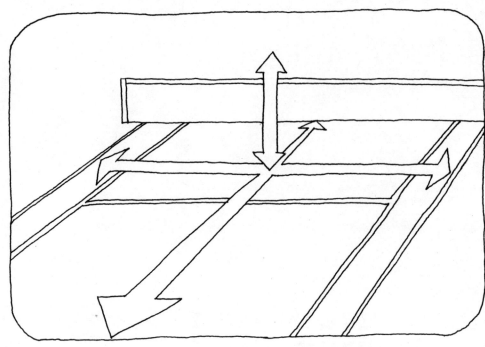

35. HIT CROSSCOURT

The safest shot from the backcourt is a crosscourt one (left) because it gives you the greatest area of court to aim at. A down-the-line shot (right) has a much narrower target area (white area) and more chance of going out of court.

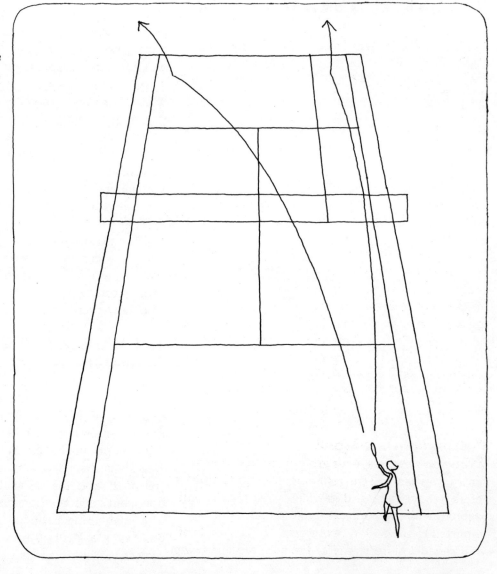

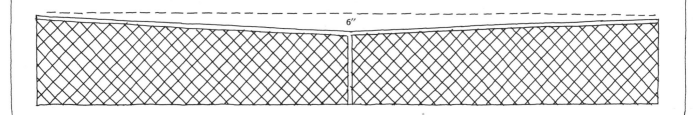

6"

short so you can attack or force him into making an error.

There are three ways to move a player: from side to side, forward and back, and up and down (see illustration #34). Let's talk about side-to-side movement first.

The first thing you need is consistent depth. What you're trying to do is keep your opponent off balance by hitting the ball deep to the left side and then deep to the right side, away from him.

From the backcourt you can hit crosscourt as well as down the line to move your opponent around. You don't have to hit the corners to make winners.

The safest shot from the maneuvering zone is crosscourt, because you have the greatest amount of court to hit into (see illustration #35). Your margin for error is much less on the shot down the line because if your aim is just a little off, you can hit out of court. The crosscourt shot is also safer for another reason. The net is six inches lower at the center than it is at the net posts (see illustration #36). So a lower shot has a better chance of clearing the net at the center than at the sides.

Putting spin on the ball

When you can place your ground strokes consistently, you can add the refinements of spin. Spin refers to how much and in which direction the ball revolves while traveling through the air. Spin is imparted to the ball in two ways: (1) the angle of your racquet at impact; (2) the path of your swing.

36. AIM ABOVE THE CENTER OF THE NET
Aim most balls above the center of the net because the net is six inches lower at this point. This gives you a much better margin of error.

37. HOW THE FACE AFFECTS SPIN

If the racquet face points up in an "open" position (left), the ball will spin counterclockwise with slight underspin (see small arrow). If the racquet face is square to the net (center), the ball will leave the racquet with relatively no spin. If the racquet face points down in a "closed" position (right), the ball will spin clockwise with slight overspin (see small arrow).

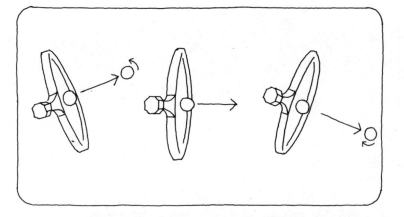

To understand how spin works, look at the ball and racquet from the side as shown in *illustration #37.* First, the ball will spin in the direction your racquet is facing. If the racquet is facing up, the ball will come off the racquet face spinning in a clockwise direction as the player sees the ball. This is called backspin, or underspin. If the racquet face is angled down, the ball will come off the racquet face spinning in a counterclockwise direction. This is called overspin or topspin.

Second, if the path of the swing is from down to up—for example, from knee level up to shoulder level—the ball will come off the racquet face spinning in a counterclockwise direction, with overspin. If the path of your swing is from up to down—for example, from shoulder height to below your waist—the ball will come off the racquet face spinning in a clockwise direction, with backspin (*see illustration #38*).

The path of your swing will have much more to do with the amount of spin than with the angle of your racquet. In other words, if you want to put a lot of overspin on the ball, you must swing up and over the ball. And, if you want to put maximum backspin on the ball, you must swing downward and underneath the ball.

If your swing is entirely level, but angled either up or down, you will impart a lesser degree of spin

38. HOW THE SWING AFFECTS SPIN

Most of the spin you put on the ball depends on the path of your swing. To put topspin on the ball, start below the ball and swing upward (left). This will put clockwise spin, or overspin (see arrows), on the ball. To put underspin on your ball, start above the flight of the ball and swing downward (right). This will put counter-clockwise spin, or backspin (see arrows), on the ball.

Topspin | Underspin

to the ball than by swinging in either an upward or a downward path. The angle of the racquet is very important, however, in helping you control the trajectory of the shot. When the racquet is angled upward, it is called an open racquet position. When it is angled downward it is called a closed racquet position (see *illustration #37*).

So, to put spin on your shots, use your normal ground strokes, but for a topspin forehand, start your racquet from below the flight of the ball and finish higher. This will make the ball rotate forward and cause it to drop faster into your opponent's court.

For underspin, start the swing from above the ball and finish lower. This makes the ball rotate backwards. Underspin takes some of the speed off the ball because it stays on the racquet longer. It's useful when you want to hit a short ball to force your opponent to come in.

Playing the ball

Once you've put some polish on your ground strokes by controlling direction and spin, you can further refine your strokes by taking the ball early—that is, before the ball has reached the top of its bounce. This has two advantages: you can play the ball sooner and get better court position and you can hit more balls at waist level.

Naturally, there are disadvantages. If you hit the ball on the way up—before it reaches the top of its bounce—you have to produce your shot a little faster and you have to control the racquet and ball at a more difficult angle.

Ultimately, you'll want to be able to hit a ball at any place after its bounce—on the rise, at the top of the bounce, or even from a slightly dropped position. The ability to handle the ball at any point after the bounce will allow you always to take the shot at waist-level where you can put maximum leverage into your swing.

I do think it's best for a small child to wait for the ball to come down to his or her waist level—at least at first. If a beginner waits to see where the ball will fall, it gives him more time.

Sometimes I wonder whether it wouldn't be nice to have a smaller tennis court for smaller people, as they do in Little League baseball. But I am constantly amazed at how quickly young persons adapt. They're not as conscious of the net being "higher" as you would imagine. Youngsters like Clint, for instance, have a great ability to isolate the ball on their side of the court and forget about what's going on on the other side. I wish that some adults I teach could do the same thing. They spend too much time worrying about what their opponents are doing and too much time looking to see where they're going to hit the ball. If they could isolate

39. TWO-HANDED BACKHAND
Players who lack power and control on their backhands can use two hands to grip the racquet, although it will cut down on their reach. Remember to use a good backhand grip with your regular hitting hand when doing this.

the ball on their side of the net as the youngsters can, they'd make cleaner contact with the ball.

Two-handed backhand

One other refinement is the two-handed backhand. This stroke is becoming popular now, especially with youngsters who are starting out. They don't have the strength to keep the racquet head up so they use two hands to get the feeling of racquet and body moving together (*see illustration #39*). When you're using two hands on a backhand, be sure to use a proper grip change so you can release the racquet head into the ball. Those players who use a forehand grip with both hands are frequently just guiding the ball through with their left hand and end up with a shortened left-handed shot (this is for right-handers). Children learning the two-handed backhand should start with a normal backhand grip and then place their free hand on the racquet in a comfortable way.

The key is to control the racquet with the hitting hand. The advantages of the two-handed shot are added power and control with the second hand. The limitation to the shot is that you have to be quicker on your feet because you've cut down on your reach.

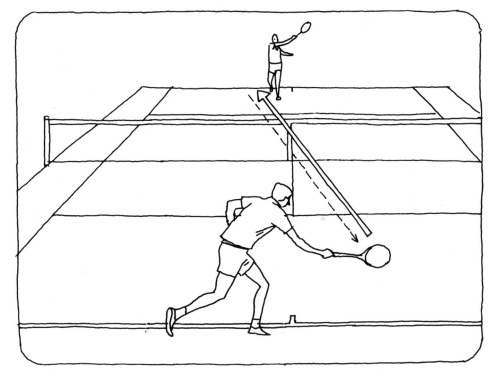

40. THE EASIEST RETURN
The easiest way to return any shot (dotted line) is to send it back the way it came, on the same line of flight (solid line).

Return of serve

The return of serve requires a few additional refinements to your ground strokes. However, the primary objective in returning a serve is to make sure the ball goes back over the net. Unless you keep the ball in play, no refinement in the world is going to help you. Don't think ahead of yourself and forget this primary goal.

Where should you stand to receive serve? Find a comfortable position where you can catch the ball with your hands. If you can catch the ball in your hands you can catch it on your racquet. Start at the baseline and then move up or back from that position, depending on the speed and direction of your opponent's serve. It's important on a first serve, especially, to place yourself directly in the line of your opponent's strongest serve so that you don't have to move very far to return it. If possible, position yourself so you don't have to take more than one step to return the ball.

The sooner you can tell whether you'll return with a forehand or backhand, and how fast the serve is coming, the better you will be able to return service. To help you "read" your opponent's serve, watch the ball as it comes off his or her racquet.

As soon as you realize the ball's direction, turn your shoulders and step to the ball.

The faster the serve, the less time you have to prepare. If you don't have much time, you may have to block the ball. By blocking the ball, I mean that you simply put your racquet face in the path of the ball, using hardly any backswing. The ball will bounce off your racquet face just as if it were a wall.

The first objective, you'll recall, is to return the ball back in play. The easiest way to do this is to return the serve on the same line of flight that it came to you (see *illustration #40*). You also want to return the serve as deep as you can, so keep a firm grip and hit the ball so it clears the net by at least three feet.

If your opponent follows his serve to the net, you want to return the ball lower so that he must volley up on the ball or you want to change the direction of the return so your opponent will have to stop and move to reach one side or the other.

Lob

The lob is a very practical shot that gets the ball over the head of your opponent at net. It forces

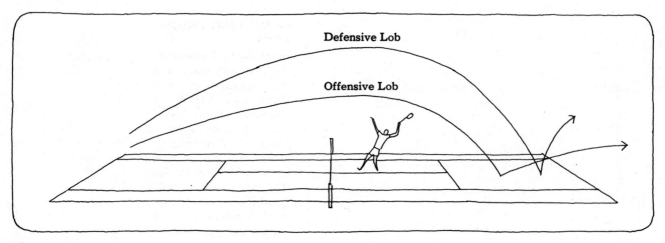

Defensive Lob

Offensive Lob

41. USING THE LOB
A defensive lob is hit high from the backcourt to land deep in your opponent's court (top). The offensive lob should just clear your opponent's racquet, drop quickly and bounce away so that he cannot scramble and return the shot.

him away from the net and also gives you time to recover for your next shot. Generally, the lob is a defensive shot, although it's possible to hit an offensive lob. A good defensive lob can be the deciding factor between two players of otherwise equal ability. So, it's an important refinement in your game.

A defensive lob has a high arc and bounces deep in your opponent's court. The highest point of its arc should be over his head (*see illustration #41*).

The defensive lob is a slow shot that requires "touch." Despite the delicacy of the shot, it should never be made with a loose wrist. Like any other ground stroke the lob requires a firm wrist and a firmly held racquet.

Start your racquet below the ball and finish high. If you can envision the face of a clock, you would start at 4 o'clock. Then with the face of your racquet open, you follow through to about 11 o'clock, still with a firm grip (*see illustration #42*). The open racquet face gives you a little underspin for better control.

The defensive lob can be hit off the forehand or backhand sides. Practice the backhand lob more because you will have an opportunity to hit more backhand lobs. That's because your opponents will often attack your backhand side and you'll have to defend on that side.

When you can hit a defensive lob that always clears the racquet of your opponent by a good margin and lands deep in his court, you should begin to experiment with using the lob as an offensive weapon. An offensive lob is a low lob that just clears your opponent's racquet head. When the ball bounces, its trajectory causes it to bounce lower toward the back fence than a defensive lob. The offensive lob should begin at 4 o'clock and finish at

12

9

3

6

Defensive Lob

42. HITTING YOUR LOBS

In hitting both offensive and defensive lobs, think of starting your stroke at about four o'clock, as indicated in these drawings. For the defensive lob (left), which sails high over your opponent's head, you should follow through at about 11 o'clock. For the offensive lob (below), which is hit low so it just clears your opponent's racquet, follow through at about 10 o'clock.

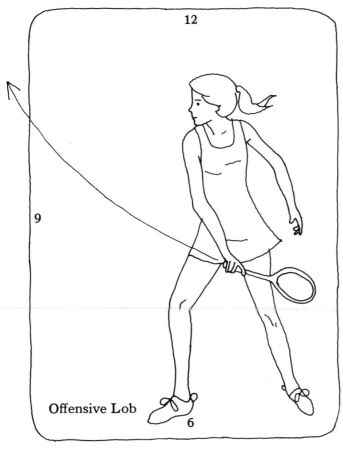

12

9

6

Offensive Lob

43. THE HALF VOLLEY
The half volley is a diffi-cult shot played close to the ground. Bend your knees to get down to the ball, watch the ball care-fully and keep a firm grip.

10 o'clock. The offensive lob can be hit with slight underspin, but this shot can be retrieved on occasion. The best offensive lobs are hit with heavy topspin. Done properly, there's almost no way that your opponent can chase down such a lob. The only disadvantage is that this is a very difficult shot and you must have complete racquet head control.

Both offensive and defensive lobs should be hit so that the highest point of the arc is over your opponent's head (*see illustration #41*).

If a lob arches too far over your head and you are forced to run back and retrieve it, the best return is a lob. You may have seen pros race back for a lob and pound it back for a dramatic passing shot. That may be correct for them, in the circumstances, but your progress as a player depends on playing the highest percentage shot, in this case a lob return. Your opponent will probably be coming in to the net behind his lob and you don't have time to turn around and check where he is. Besides, a lob is easier to hit than a powerful overhead or driving ground stroke.

THE APPROACH ZONE
Approach shots

As the level of your game improves and the caliber of your opponents gets better, you'll find that you will win more points by getting up to the net to put your opponent's returns away with crisp volleys.

However, it's more than 30 feet from the baseline to a commanding net position. It's rare for any player to be able to cover that distance between shots so you'll inevitably end up hitting one shot from the approach zone as you try to gain the net.

It is particularly helpful in playing this zone to refer back to the basics—ball sense, movement and racquet control. You must be able to anticipate a short shot, move up beside the ball so you can hit it at the top of its bounce, and control your racquet for the shorter distance required.

Top players rarely miss a ball in this zone. The average player makes mistakes in this zone because he is late in moving forward and he usually overplays the ball; he either tries to play a difficult shot or tries to win the point outright.

Your swing for approach shots should be level, like sweeping a ball off a table top. This will encourage you to return the shot straight back over the net. You want a short, compact backswing. Remember, in this zone you want to clear the net by about two feet, not three, because you are closer to it. Also, approach shots should almost always be hit down the line, rather than crosscourt. The reason is that it is quicker and easier to follow the ball's line of flight to the best volleying position. If you hit crosscourt, you would open your court for an easy passing shot.

You should play this zone with care. Use it only to improve your position and as a means to get to the putaway zone, not to win the point outright. If you find yourself in the approach zone and can hit the ball in the air, simply volley the ball deep into your opponent's court and follow the ball in to your putaway zone.

Half volley

You may find that your opponent drops a shot at your feet. It's impossible to play a conventional approach shot when the ball is close to the ground so you'll have to resort to a shot known as the half volley. A half volley is a shot that you must play almost instantly after it bounces on the court. It is not a true volley because you don't hit it in the air (see illustration #43).

You'll have little time to make this shot so it's hard to hit an effective half volley. Indeed, most top players assume that if they can make their opponent half volley, the resulting shot will be so bad that they can put it away with ease. However, there are good half volleyers like Roy Emerson, who treat the shot offensively. You can do the same.

There are three keys to a successful half volley. First, bend your knees to get your body down to the ball—very close to the ground. Stay down on the ball because if you come up, with either your body or your racquet, you'll hit the ball into the net. Second, grip the racquet as firmly as you can, with

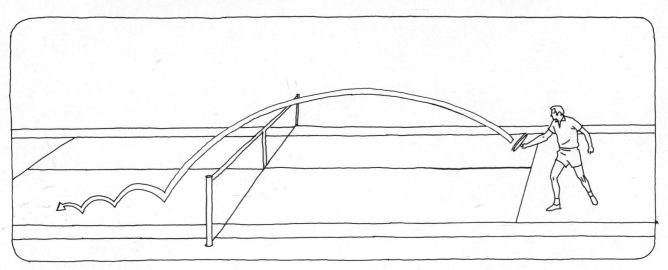

44. THE DROP SHOT

A fine touch is needed to hit a drop shot that just clears the net. When a good drop shot is not returned, it ought to bounce at least three times before it reaches the service line.

45. SLINGSHOT ACTION

The action of hitting a backhand volley is like using the fork of a slingshot. It requires a short, punching action and a firm grip.

a slightly open face. Third, hit solidly, straight through the ball with a short follow-through. Don't try to lift the ball or use topspin. Concentrate on the hitting zone itself. Use a short backswing and a brief follow-through.

Hit the ball deep down the center into the other court, if possible. Aim for the center-court area because this means the ball will pass over the center of the net at its lowest and safest part, and your opponent will have less angle for a passing shot.

Drop shot

When your opponent hits a short ball you'll be forced into the mid-court area to make your return. Now you have a choice. You can either return the ball deep and continue up to the net or you can return the ball very short into your opponent's court. To hit such a short shot you'll have to use a shot that barely drops over the net (see *illustration #44*).

A drop shot is really a mini-lob. Its primary purpose is to move your opponent forward. You hit it gently up and over the net. Because you're taking speed off the ball it's a shot that requires "touch." The drop shot is executed with a cupping motion of your swing. The perfect drop shot would probably bounce three times before it reached the service line. Don't hit a drop shot so the ball bounces first in mid-court.

Always precede a drop shot with a deep drive so that your opponent will be forced to run all the way from the baseline to the net to return your shot. Even if he gets his racquet on the ball, the resulting scrambling shot will often be easy for you to put away. Don't try a drop shot off a strong, deep drive from the maneuvering zone. Drop shots are best made from the approach zone where you have a choice of shots available.

I would never use the drop shot at a really

critical point in a match. If the shot backfires, you'll be in trouble. Treat the drop shot as a necessary but rare weapon in your repertory. Use it occasionally when you're confident of its chances of succeeding.

THE PUTAWAY ZONE
Volleys

When you begin to play at the net, you'll need a crisp, controlled volley that you can use as an offensive weapon. A good volley is a vital part of your doubles armory and an essential refinement if you want to become an aggressive singles player.

Your main concern in hitting a volley is putting the flat face of the racquet against the ball. You'll need a very firm wrist and grip to control your volleys. For this reason I recommend that you begin volleying with your normal ground stroke grips. Most top players use only one grip for volleying because they do not have time to change grips in the fast action of net play. In time you will naturally tend to use a grip somewhere between your usual forehand and backhand grips.

To hit the volley successfully you should put the racquet strings on the ball as early as possible. Always move forward to volley. Move in quickly to get into a position where you have a better choice of angles for your shot. The action of volleying is rather like catching the ball on the face of your racquet just as a baseball player would catch a ball with his glove. Do it firmly and positively and be sure that you hit the ball in the center of your racquet. Watch the ball throughout the stroke.

On the backhand side, the action of volleying is like using the fork of a slingshot. Your shoulders should come around and your hand should hold the racquet as if you were shooting a slingshot (see *illustration #45*). Be sure that you get your

46. STOP VOLLEY

A stop volley is one of the most delicate touch shots and requires careful control. You should take the speed off the volley by moving your racquet in a saucer-shaped motion. Lift the ball enough to merely cross the net and let it die.

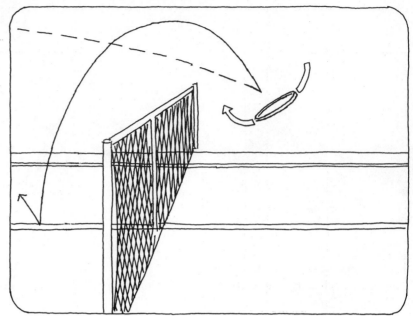

racquet head and body behind the line of flight of the ball. A full shoulder pivot will allow you to get your weight behind your backhand.

When your basic backhand and forehand volleys are in good shape you'll probably want to try a few variations like the angle, stop and reflex volleys.

The angle volley is hit diagonally into the approach zone of your opponent. To get a sharp angle you should hit the ball well out in front of you, placing it far away from your opponent.

A stop volley is the net-play equivalent of the drop shot. A stop volley is a volley that falls inside your opponent's putaway zone. It is one of the most delicate of touch shots and one which requires a great deal of practice to perfect. You must make a lighter touch with your strings by cupping and catching the ball to take the speed off it. Your racquet will move in a saucer-shaped motion (*see illustration #46*). Try your stop volleys crosscourt so that they can stay in the air a little longer and have more court to land in.

The reflex volley is used to block shots aimed directly at your body. That's simply a matter of getting your racquet head up so it will contact the ball in the center of the strings. Balls hit directly at your body are easier to return with the back-hand. Hold your wrist and grip even more firmly than usual so that the ball's speed causes it to rebound off the strings solidly enough to return into your opponent's court.

When you play the net position, you should not always remain in the center. You should move toward either side as necessary to cover the largest possible path of your opponent's return.

Think of your own baseline corners as the base

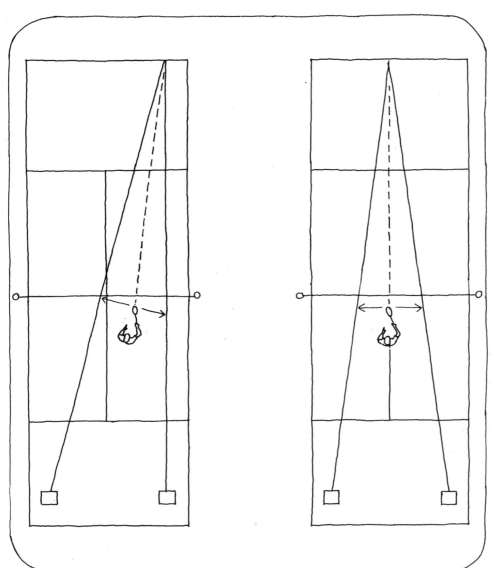

47. VOLLEY POSITION

To best position yourself for a volley, bisect the angle formed by your opponent's position at which he contacts the ball and the two base targets (white blocks) behind you. The triangle formed (white areas) represents the maximum area in which your opponent can hit. When the oncoming ball is to your right (far left), position yourself right of center. When the oncoming ball is centered, position yourself in the center of the court (right).

48. SEE THE CONTACT

In preparation for the serve, visualize the arc the racquet will follow to put the ball in play. As you raise your arm for the toss, your upper body stretches with the racquet; your weight is back (above). In the hitting zone (center, opposite page) your weight and the racquet move forward following the arc. Keep your head and chin up as you watch the strings contact the ball. In the finish (far right), your arm and weight follow through in a sweeping curve across your body as you follow the line of flight of the ball.

of a triangle, and your opponent as the apex of the triangle (*see illustration #47*). Your opponent's return has to stay within that triangle if he wants his shot to bounce in the court.

In volleying, you should always position yourself midway between the sides of that triangle; in other words, you should bisect that angle. This will guarantee you the greatest possible defense against his return. For example, if you volley deep to your opponent's backhand, you will need to move only a few feet to the right of the center line, as shown in *illustration #47*. Don't go too close to the alley because that would leave you wide open on your backhand side.

SERVE AND OVERHEAD

Though the components of a serve often sound complicated, I like to keep it simple. Just visualize the arc your racquet will swing on and lift the ball into that arc. The lift starts at shoulder level and the whole body follows upward so that, as your racquet moves through the hitting zone, your body extends to full stretch for a powerful hit. The bigger the arc is, the better your swing will be. And the better your swing, of course, the more effective your serve will become.

If you have a good visual picture of the perfect serve, everything else will be encouraged to happen naturally. When your racquet goes back, your weight will go back. When your racquet goes

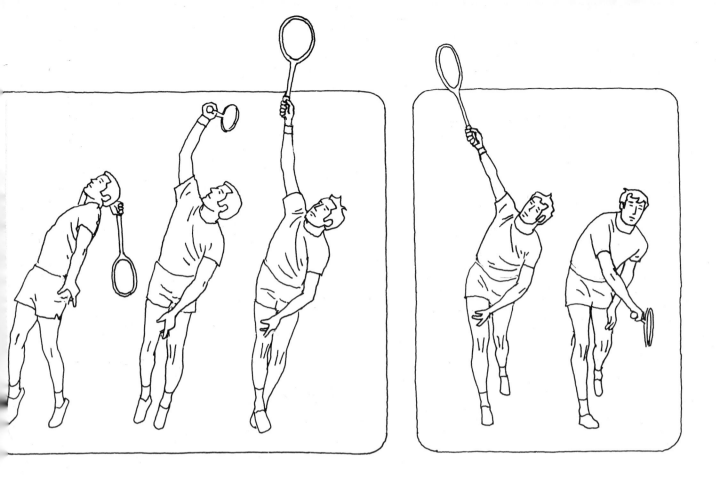

forward your weight will go forward. After the hit your racquet will continue out into the court and you'll complete the follow-through with a sweeping arc across your body. As you finish, the shoulder of your hitting arm should point in the direction of your serve. Be certain that you keep your head and chin up while watching the strings make contact with the ball (*see illustration #48*).

Preparation begins with position. In singles, stand within three feet of the center line. The reason for standing near the center is that after you've hit the serve, you're in a better court position to play the next shot. In doubles, stand farther away from the center—about six to seven feet—for the same reason.

The forward foot should be pointed in the general direction of the net post on your right, if you're a right-hander (the left net post if you are a left-hander). This gives you the ability to keep the foot stationary while still permitting rotation of your hips and shoulders. If your front foot were perpendicular or parallel to the baseline, it would restrict your backswing and, as a result, your power.

When you wish to refine your serve, you should keep the basic ideas in mind and add to them gradually. Every good serve has a good toss. The toss doesn't have to be more than a few feet high after leaving your hand. A common mistake is to toss the ball too high, which means you'll have to hit a falling ball. This will interrupt the timing of

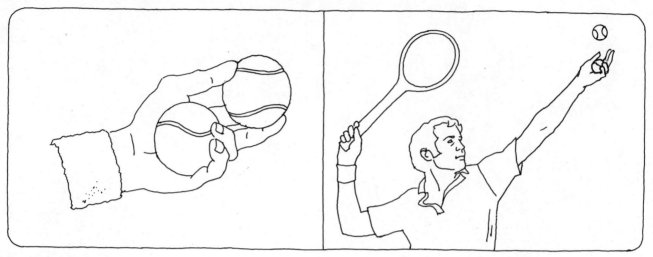

49. RELEASE THE BALL GENTLY
Hold the ball in the tips of your fingers (left) and open them to release the ball gently (right).

your serve and cause a hitch in your swing. You don't throw the ball up; you release the ball (*see illustration #49*). The upward lift of your arm offers sufficient momentum. As you toss, get the feeling that your upper body is stretching and lengthening (*see illustration #50*).

The lift is the first forward motion you make. As your racquet drops behind your back, the release of the ball should pull you into the direction you are going to serve into the court. If you allowed the ball to fall from its peak without hitting it, it would fall about a foot inside the court into an area the size of your racquet face (*see illustration #51*). The taller the player, the farther out the ball should fall. Tossing into the court ensures that you'll reach into the ball. Don't go so far out that you have to chase it, though.

Other common serving errors occur when the toss is poorly timed. If you're hitting the ball late on the serve, for instance, it will probably go out. You've let the ball fall on your racquet when it's not in a hitting position. If you're hitting the ball early, it means that your racquet's already been at the top and it's hitting the ball on the way down. The ball will probably go into the net. Corrections can be made simply by pulling your toss back and adjusting your timing. Many players swing a little faster or hit a little harder when their serves are "off." Don't do that. All you'll do is throw your timing off even more.

If your timing is good but your direction is bad, check your serving position. If the ball isn't going where you want it to, it's just a matter of adjustment. You get your basic direction from your feet and your racquet head, not from trying to aim the ball. Move your feet around to alter your serving direction. Spread your feet at least the width of

50. STRETCH FOR THE BALL

As you raise your arm to toss the ball, get the feeling that your whole upper body is stretching and lengthening.

51. AIM FOR CONSISTENCY

If you were to let the ball fall from the peak of its toss without hitting it, the ball should fall about a foot in front of you. If your toss is consistent, the ball will drop within an area no bigger than the face of your racquet.

52. DIRECTING YOUR SERVE

To change the direction of your serve, alter the position of your back foot, not the front, with your feet about shoulder-width apart. A line drawn along your toes will indicate the direction your serve will go.

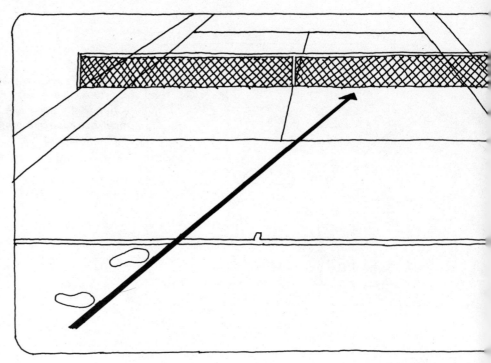

your shoulders. The line across the toes of both feet should point where you want to hit the ball (*see illustration #52*). To change direction, move the back foot, not the front foot.

Once the ball's in motion, you just release the racquet head. In other words, once you've released the racquet head, you've "thrown" it. Any time you try to guide it, or "massage" it by rolling around on the ball instead of hitting it cleanly, it's because you're not following through correctly.

I like to let beginners and intermediates practice serving without using a ball. If I can hear the air go through the racquet, I know that they're swinging with good acceleration. If I don't hear it, it means that they're probably pushing it. Another good serving drill is to practice throwing the ball without a racquet. Take your position at the baseline and throw the ball into the opposite service court. This is a particularly good drill for learning direction of your serves.

The arc of the racquet head will take over the direction of the ball—if you finish the serve. The racquet follows the line of flight all the way onto the court and down to the left-hand side of your body. Exaggerate it! The more exaggerated the follow-through, the more control you're going to have on your serve.

Foot faults

In serving, you want to stand far enough from the center line and behind the baseline to avoid any problem with foot-faulting. A foot fault is touching either of these lines before the racquet hits the ball.

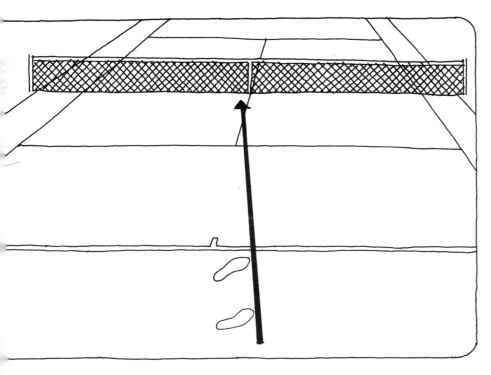

53. FOOT FAULTS

The three most common foot faults during the serve are stepping over the center line (left), touching the baseline (center) and stepping over the baseline before hitting the ball (right). Committing one of these faults on the first serve requires a second serve; if it happens on your second serve, you lose the point.

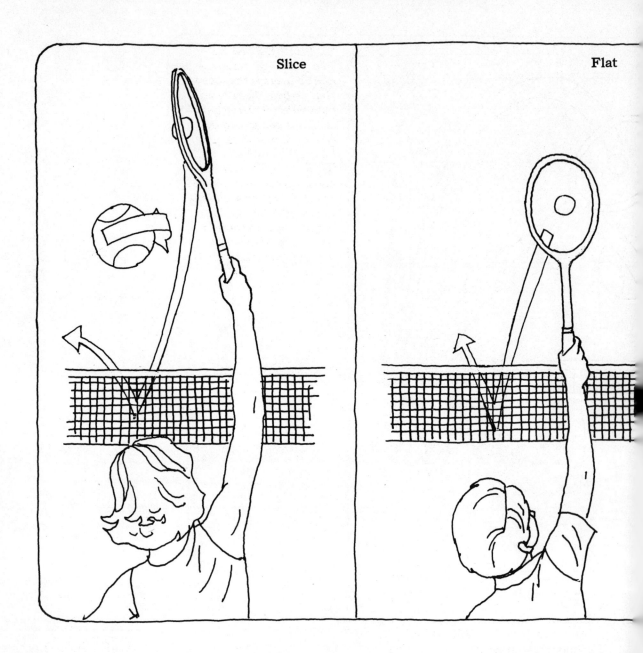

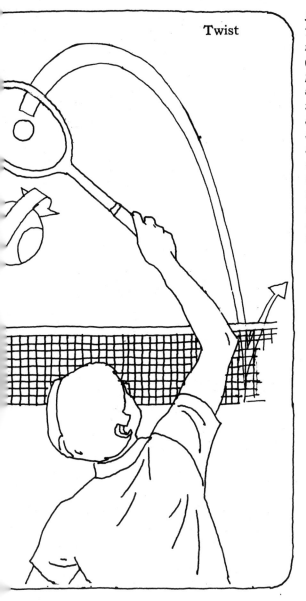
Twist

54. THREE SERVES
The workhorse serve for most players is the slice (left) where the racquet puts sidespin on the ball, so that it bounces to the receiver's right. You should also learn the flat serve (center) for speed and an occasional change of pace. The twist serve is the most difficult; the racquet applies topspin that makes the ball take higher bounces and swerve to the receiver's left.

The most common foot fault is when your left foot steps on the baseline just before your racquet hits the ball (*see illustration #53*). It is also a foot fault if your right foot crosses the baseline and touches the ground before the serve is hit. Another foot fault is also shown in *illustration #53*.

Slice serve
There are several types of spin serves. One is the slice, which involves a natural throwing motion and where the ball moves off your racquet with just enough spin to control it easily. Another is the twist, which makes the ball bounce a little higher (*see illustration #54*).

I recommend the slice serve for the majority of players because it is the most natural way to control spin and direction. You'll need a good toss at least a foot in front of your right shoulder, and your follow-through should be exaggerated from right to

left (the reverse if you are left-handed) across your body.

The spin is applied by the angle of the strings on impact and the follow-through across the body. On the natural slice, stroke the ball at about 2 o'clock (assuming that the ball is a face of a clock facing the server). A severely angled racquet will put more "bite" into the ball for more spin. The slice serve will bounce to your left (the receiver's right), assuming you are right-handed. If you impart more spin, you should aim higher over the net and follow through as far as possible.

You can adjust the speed and direction of the slice serve more easily than any of the others. It's the easiest on you physically while it's also the most difficult for an opponent to read. When you mix serving speeds or add spin or take spin off so that some bounce higher and some not so high, you'll keep your opponents guessing all the time.

Flat serve

The flat serve is hit with a flat racquet face and at the maximum height you can stretch. This combination gives you the maximum speed of any serve, which is why the flat serve is often referred to as the cannonball.

The use of this serve is restricted to an occasional ace, or as a change of pace. In a match, I use a flat serve sparingly to either set up my opponent for a slower serve or to win a quick point.

The reason this serve is not used more frequently is that it is hit so fast that it demands minimum clearance over the net. Obviously, the closer to the net I have to hit, the less chance I have of clearing it. Thus the flat serve is much less consistent and is a relatively low percentage serve.

The toss and preparation for the flat serve are the same as for the slice serve. The only difference in the hitting zone is that you must turn the face of the racquet so that it meets the ball flat and from directly behind the center of the ball. The motion is an exaggerated overhand swing with the finish going straight out and then down across your body.

Twist serve

Once you have mastered the flat and slice serves, you can add a third variety to your repertory— the twist or topspin serve. The twist is an advanced serve. It curves high over the net but bounces away to your right (the receiver's left) into the backcourt (*see illustration #54*).

The twist serve is used primarily as a second serve, or as a first serve in doubles because it's easy to get it in the service court. It is also used as a first serve when you plan to serve and volley. But you must be sure to aim high over the net because the topspin causes the twist serve to drop sharply.

In the twist serve, you toss the ball slightly lower than for a slice serve. The toss should still be in front of your body, not behind your head, so your serve will penetrate your opponent's court. The old version of the twist serve is really a "kick" serve; it calls for a toss more behind your head which gives it more spin but not much forward motion. In other words, it "kicks" higher but doesn't penetrate enough to keep your opponent from attacking it.

To prepare for the twist, your racquet drops as low as possible behind your back in an exaggerated back-scratching position. This will give you the momentum you need to apply maximum topspin. To hit the twist serve, your racquet comes up and over the ball with a glancing motion, almost as if you were brushing the racquet over the top of the ball. This is why the toss is lower. You will make contact before you get to full stretch.

In using the twist serve, you're running a risk because the ball has to glance off your racquet. You have to be quite a talented player to be able to control it. I would not recommend the topspin

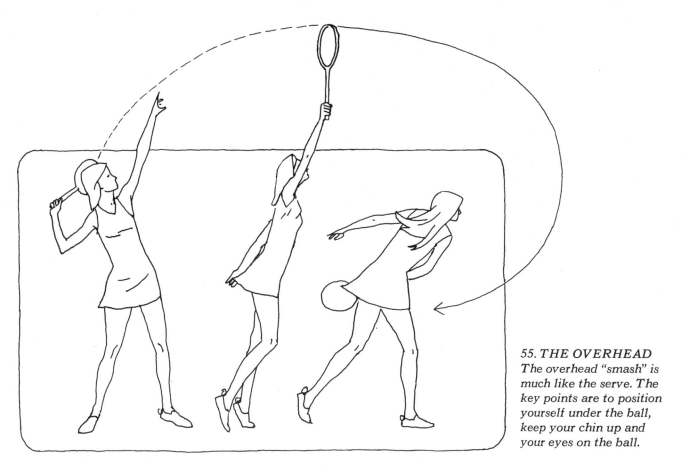

55. THE OVERHEAD
The overhead "smash" is much like the serve. The key points are to position yourself under the ball, keep your chin up and your eyes on the ball.

serve for a beginner. I would suggest you stick to the slice serve.

Overhead

The overhead is a ball hit in the air above your head. It is a shot hit in response to a lob. The overhead is a close cousin to the serve. They have the same hitting zone and a similar finish. To prepare for an overhead get the racquet behind your head to begin the same arc as you would use to serve (*see illustration #55*).

For the overhead, you must turn your side to the net and maneuver yourself under the ball. As soon as you realize you are going to hit an overhead, move your right foot back (your left foot if you are a left-hander) and slide to the correct position under the ball. To help you judge the ball, you should reach a position under the ball so that if you reached up with your left hand you'd be able to catch the ball.

At the same time you aim with your left arm, your racquet head should be placed into the back-scratching position. Then step forward with your left foot, reach up and hit the ball at full stretch just as you would hit a serve. Finish out and across your body. The overhead will normally be hit a little flatter than your serve.

The technique for the overhead is relatively easy. The major difficulty usually comes in timing the shot. To improve your timing, keep your chin up

and your eyes on the ball through the hitting zone.

On a very high lob, let the ball bounce. You don't want to hit the ball before it bounces because it is more difficult to judge and time your shot. On these high lobs, be sure to position yourself at least 10 feet behind the spot the ball will hit. This will give you time to step into the ball and swing comfortably.

It's more important to place an overhead shot than to try to kill it. If you're going to try to put the ball out of your opponent's reach, you'll want to hit it at three-quarter speed, though sometimes you'll find you're not quite comfortable doing that. A good overhead smash is just a matter of putting the strings on the ball and moving your racquet head enough for a good finish. Basically, all that's necessary is to hit the ball faster than your opponent can move. Younger players should be thinking of this, especially, so they won't overhit. It's fun to kill the easy one, but don't overdo it.

CORRECTING YOUR SWING FAULTS

When you have a clear understanding of what it takes to hit any tennis shot, that there are but three elements common to every stroke—preparation, hitting zone and finish—you can correct your own mistakes. Almost anyone can spot a fault, but not everyone can tell you what caused the fault. Always the fault can be found in one of the three elements of the swing: the preparation, the hitting

56. DON'T HIT LATE
A common swing fault is hitting late. This is the result of poor timing in your preparation. Be sure to hit the ball in front of your body to prevent a wristy shot and a weak return.

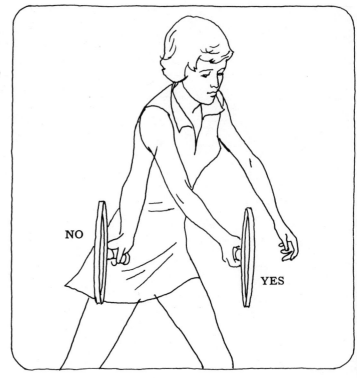

NO

YES

zone or the finish.

If there is a flaw in the swing, look first at your preparation. The majority of poor shots are the result of poor preparation. So on ground strokes check to see that your racquet has completed a backswing on the line of flight of the oncoming ball; then check that you have turned side-on to the net and your weight is on the back foot. Remember, start early and don't rush your preparation.

If you're not hitting with enough power, it's probably because you don't have enough backswing; that is, you're not reaching back far enough. If you just pull it back another six inches or so, the racquet can pick up more momentum as it comes through and give you more power. If you're hitting late or find yourself rushing in the hitting zone, you probably have too much backswing.

What I'm getting at here is to emphasize that the method of hitting the ball is not as important as the fact that every good ground stroke needs to have a proper backswing for control, for power and for good depth. But keep it comfortable. Your arm doesn't have to be completely straight or extended, just enough freedom of arm to give you the backswing that's necessary.

If everything checks out in your preparation, check your hitting zone. In this area, most errors are caused by poor timing—that is, you will hit late (behind your body) or early (before the ball gets to you). You might notice a tendency to get wristy. That will indicate that you are hitting late. If you

hit early, you are not stepping in the direction you want to hit. In other words, your racquet moves forward before your body does (*see illustration #56*). Remember, in the hitting zone you must always watch the strings hit the ball.

If you checked out in the first two, the error is in your finish. You are fortunate if the error is here because it's easy to correct. Simply keep your forward foot in place until your shot clears the net. The most common error here is rushing to recover too quickly to get to the next shot. Just remember to complete your shot before you move off for the next one. There's no place to recover to if you miss the shot and hit it into the net.

Here's a little tip that helps me tremendously when I run into a bad spell of serving. If you are making a bad swing, think of your toss. If you are making a bad toss, think of your swing. I think you'll find that concentrating on making a good toss will immediately improve your swing, and vice versa.

CHECKPOINTS FOR BAD SHOTS

At this point let me give you a few checkpoints that will help you on the court. If your shots are flying high and out of court, you are either hitting late or the racquet strings are facing upward. So, first lower your sights and then square the racquet face. If your shots are consistently hitting the net, you are either hitting too early or your racquet is facing downward. In this case, raise your sights and square your racquet. If your shots glance to the side of the court, you are hitting either too early or too late. When this happens, check to see that your racquet face is parallel to the net on impact.

You may be asking yourself, "What about the knees, the hips, and the other parts of the body?" Don't! That just confuses the issue. Top players seldom think about these details. The worst thing you can do is think too much about wrists, elbows, shoulders, hips and so forth instead of emphasizing the racquet head. If you're having problems with your wrists, for example, it's probably because your timing is not good. I'd rather emphasize the *cause* of a wristy shot. This could stem from hitting late because you prepared late or because your grip wasn't firm enough to allow your racquet head to move through as fast as the oncoming ball.

For example, if you are hitting late, try to hit the ball a little sooner, about a foot in front of you (nearer the net). As long as you're making contact in the correct hitting zone, you'll find that the racquet head will just sweep through and the wrist will act as a hinge on a door, opening and closing firmly on the ball.

Or it might be because your racquet was off the line of flight and the only way you could adjust was by breaking your wrist. I don't like to get a person so conscious of his wrist he doesn't think of the real cause: racquet head control. If I can get that reasoning across, I'll be happy.

You may be tempted, after reading this chapter, to run out and try everything at once. Unless you're a very advanced player, give yourself time to learn the different shots. You will develop a more solid game if you take gradual steps.

Don't let the fact that you can't hit one type of shot hinder your progress. You can still improve your game, even though it contains some weakness. Always play around the weakness. If a certain type of shot is difficult for you to learn (it might be the overhead, the backhand or the volley), forget that shot and go on to learn others.

Find your strength. It might be your forehand or your serve. Use that strength in playing. Gradually, you'll gain the experience and racquet sense to hit the shots that give you trouble.

RETURNING SERVE FROM THE MANEUVERING ZONE

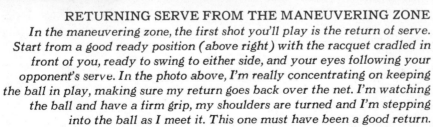

In the maneuvering zone, the first shot you'll play is the return of serve. Start from a good ready position (above right) with the racquet cradled in front of you, ready to swing to either side, and your eyes following your opponent's serve. In the photo above, I'm really concentrating on keeping the ball in play, making sure my return goes back over the net. I'm watching the ball and have a firm grip, my shoulders are turned and I'm stepping into the ball as I meet it. This one must have been a good return.

LOBBING FROM
THE MANEUVERING ZONE

The lob is a great weapon from the maneuvering zone. The offensive lob I'm hitting here is a big factor in my recent success because I can disguise it until the last moment. I get my racquet below the ball with a firm wrist so I have the option of slicing under it or putting topspin on the ball. This is a low lob, and on the follow-through I want to put just enough height on the shot to clear my opponent's head (and racquet) at the net.

APPROACH ZONE SHOTS

The approach shot is necessary if you want to advance your game. How well you play in the approach zone is the real test of a player's ability. When you leave the baseline to work your way to the net, your approach shots require a shorter backswing (top left and bottom left), a swing that is *level to the ground and a controlled finish (top right and bottom right). Even though you are coming in toward the net, I suggest you slow down, or even stop to steady your body just before impact, at least until you have a lot of experience in the approach zone.*

THE VOLLEY AND THE HALF VOLLEY

Angie is hitting a mid-court forehand volley above, a frequent necessity in the approach zone. Her crossover footwork is good. She must watch the ball, keep low and have a firm grip. In the photo at right, I have been caught in the mid-court and forced to half volley—hitting the ball on a very short hop. The half volley is difficult for most players because they never practice it. My concentration is on bending down to the ball, keeping my grip very firm, my racquet flat and my head down so I can watch the ball as it ricochets off the court into my racquet.

PUT AWAY THE SHOT AT THE NET

The reason you come in to the net, the putaway zone, is to win the point, and almost every shot here is played in the air. At far left, I'm preparing for an overhead, moving into mid-court as I position myself for contact. In the smaller picture at left, John is showing me the correct position for the forehand volley, one of my weaknesses. Below, I'm hitting a backhand volley, one of my strengths. John feels that I choke up too much on the grip; but notice that I keep the racquet head above the wrist for good leverage and the ball is contacting the center of the strings. In the bottom photos, John hits a forehand volley, one of his favorite shots and a consistent winner when he's hot.

THE FLAT SERVE

Angie is demonstrating the flat serve. Notice that she holds two balls in her left hand for her toss. The first she will release from her fingertips; the second is held in the palm of the hand to give a support. Her ready position is good for the flat serve. The basic toss and timing seem to be perfect. As she winds up to serve, her weight and the racquet are moving back and the toss is going up. The toss is the first forward motion of the serve, and her racquet will come directly overhead with the racquet face meeting the ball absolutely facing (parallel to) the net. The motion comes straight overhand and follows down to the left side of the body.

My slice serve (above) is a basic serve and it should be your basic serve. The key to a good slice serve is in the preparation. My racquet and weight move back as my toss goes up. The ball toss is made with a light release from my fingertips. I hit the ball at full stretch. My racquet slices into the ball at approximately 2 o'clock if you're looking into the face of a clock. This puts bite on the shot. Note that the follow-through is exaggerated to my left side.

The twist or topspin serve is definitely an advanced shot. In singles, I use this for a second serve to get the maximum clearance over the net. I frequently use it in doubles as a first serve so I can follow the ball in. The two key differences between the twist and the slice serves are shown at left. First, I must allow my racquet to drop low on the backswing (left) so that I can get a good knee bend and spring up and into the ball. Second, the hitting action is more of a brushing motion over the top of the ball to get a maximum spin or bite. Some players finish on the right side of the body. My follow-through starts to my right but actually ends up on the left side of my body.

THE SLICE AND TWIST SERVES

The two closeup views below show the key difference between the slice (top) and twist (bottom) serves at the critical moment before impact. You will notice in the top picture that the racquet is in position to slice across the outside of the ball, whereas in the twist serve the racquet is in position to come up and over the top of the ball.

CHAPTER 5: PLAYING TO WIN

I like to think of strategy as the way to win. There are many ways to win a tennis match. As your game develops, you will be able to call on more and more of them.

In this chapter, I want to show you the strategies you can use at your present level and how you can advance as your stroking improves and your experience increases. To be a better student of the game, you should realize the elements that go into strategy. Those elements begin with the playing conditions—weather, lighting, background and speed of the court. Another is knowing your opponent and his ability and anticipating his moves. Third, and possibly most important, is the style of your play. Use this knowledge to find a way to win.

KNOW YOUR OPPONENT

The basic element of strategy is to know your opponent. As quickly as you can, learn what his abilities are, what shots he hits best, which zones of the court he prefers and which he does not. Here's something you can try: hang up a very easy ball over your opponent's mid-court, preferably on his forehand side, and see what he does with it. If he puts the ball away and controls it adequately, you know to stay away from that side. If he can't handle it well, you'll know there is some weakness there. By giving your opponent an easy shot, you can find out his strengths and weaknesses pretty quickly.

Many players can hit one shot or two, but not three or four shots in a row. The more shots you return, the tighter they get. Some players move better from side to side than they do forward and back. You should look for these weaknesses in your

57. WRONG FOOTING
When your opponent begins to anticipate your side-to-side shots, you have an opportunity to catch him off guard and force an error. Switch your pattern so that the ball lands behind him and traps him on the wrong foot. He'll have to struggle to recatch his balance and probably will hit an awkward return shot.

opponent's mental and physical makeup, just as you look for weaknesses in his strokes.

ANTICIPATION

Another vital element of strategy is anticipation— knowing what to expect on a given shot and in a given situation. Anticipation comes with experience, but you can anticipate some things from the very beginning, simply because they are logical. Here are a few examples:

● A strong serve hit directly at a player should bring a weak return. If you anticipate a weak return, you can prepare to make an approach shot.

● If you hit into a wide-open court and your opponent must run to retrieve your shot, you can reasonably anticipate a weak return and thus prepare to move up.

● If your opponent hits a deep shot to your backhand, you might expect his next shot to come to your forehand in an attempt to run you back and forth.

● If you must run up for a short shot, you'd be smart to anticipate that your opponent would hit a lob or passing shot to an open area of court.

Use your opponent's anticipation to your advantage. When you move him rapidly from side to side, he'll start to anticipate your next shot. That's the time to cross him up and either hit a short shot, or return it in the same direction he's just played from. In either case, he'll have to stop and change direction abruptly.

The better you can anticipate, the quicker you will progress to a higher level of play. Anticipating

correctly can save a step or two, which is often the difference between winning and losing the point. Winning an extra point or two is often the margin in a close match.

SINGLES STRATEGY

There is no one perfect strategy for singles play. In fact, strategy will change from set to set as the match progresses. There are three basic styles of play: 1) the backcourt game; 2) the serve and volley game, and 3) the all-court game. It is interesting to me to identify the favorite style of play of the player using it. Show me a conservative person, and I'll show you a backcourt specialist, while the restless person wants to play the serve and volley game. It takes a well-disciplined, well-coached player to conquer the all-court game; it is the ultimate goal in tennis.

Backcourt play

All play starts from the backcourt, so you might consider this the foundation of your game. A backcourt player stays mostly on the baseline and trades deep drives with his opponent. It is the style of play that most beginners adopt naturally, because they have more time to hit the ball. Let me say quickly, however, that the backcourt is not for beginners only. Chris Evert, Bjorn Borg and Nancy Gunter, for example, are basically backcourt players whose aggressive ground strokes have taken them to the top in competitive tennis.

Backcourt players develop sound ground strokes. Their serve is used mainly to get the opponent off

balance. The basic tactic in playing from the
baseline is to hit most of your shots crosscourt. Your
margin of error is greater than hitting down the line
since you have more court to aim for and you will
be hitting over the lowest part of the net. If you can
hit deep and crosscourt, you will be able to pull
your opponent out of court and force him to make a
weak return. Make your opponent move by hitting
away from him as much as possible. However,
beware of simply alternating shots to either side of
the court. Chances are your opponent will develop a
rhythm and begin to anticipate your shots. That's
when you should hit a shot behind your opponent to
catch him on the wrong foot. He'll have to turn
around and make an awkward shot or forced error
(see *illustration #57*). Don't rush a point, but
groove your shot so that your opponent is forced
into committing an error, or hitting from an
awkward position.

When playing against a backcourt player, be as
patient as he is. Vary your shots to break the rhythm
of the point. Most backcourt players come up to the
net only when *they* want to; make them come in
when *you* want them to, before they are ready.
Bring your opponent to the net by hitting a deep
ball and then a short angle, or even drop shot.
Finally, you might figure a way to work your way
in to the net and volley. Don't rush, because the
backcourt player can lob and may have good
control of his passing shots.

With faster courts and equipment, men generally
do not rely on the baseline game to win. However,
most women play their tennis from the backcourt.

They feel they have better control of their ground strokes than their volleys, so they are more comfortable in playing the steadier backcourt game.

It is a must for young players to develop sound shots in the backcourt area before moving into the other styles. My coach insisted that I learn all of the shots from the baseline, including passing shots and lobs, before I moved on to learn others. He gave me the same fundamental shots at age 12 that I use today from this area of the court. For all players, the backcourt game should be used to develop long, sweeping ground strokes and the ability to play both offense and defense.

Serve and volley play

If you favor an offensive style, you should improve your serve and play the serve and volley game. In this type of play, you serve deep and move in quickly to volley the return of serve deep to your opponent's court and then go to the net for a putaway. This aggressive manner of play is popular and especially effective on grass and fast surfaces. Arthur Ashe, Stan Smith and Billie Jean King are good examples of this style.

Your serve should have enough spin to control its direction and to give you time to get to a comfortable first volley position. A good three-quarter speed serve deep to your opponent's backhand should be your basic serve. You can hit into the body of the receiver or make him reach for a backhand, but the percentage serve will go in the direction of the backhand of your opponent to draw an easier ball for you to volley.

Always assume that your serve is going in and follow the line of flight to the net. Never wait to see if your serve is good. You'll be surprised at how much your serve and confidence will improve if you

follow this guideline.

On the first volley be sure to get your balance. If you are in balance, all you need to do is meet the ball in the center of your racquet and volley it deep into your opponent's court. Don't just stand there; move in. Men will find this style of play easier to master after they practice a combination of the three basic shots—the first serve, the first volley and the putaway volley.

Women will also enjoy exploring the new areas of offensive tennis and will be surprised at their ability to improve this part of their game with no additional instruction. Practice is all that it takes to add this new dimension. Most women can learn to serve and volley, but they forget to use it in competition.

Junior players must be trained to serve and volley. They should practice the same sequence mentioned above—first serve, first volley and putaway volley. On the serve, the forward motion that follows the ball to the net will encourage a good ball toss, that is, one that is made in front of the body, and will also encourage a good finish.

Run forward a few steps even after serving a fault; this will improve concentration and accuracy. Boys normally find it easy to adapt to this style and begin to put winning combinations together. Girls may not be as successful, but will improve their serves and their ability to move forward by practicing the serve and volley. They can also use this style for a surprise attack or a change of pace.

To beat the serve and volley game, you will need an effective return of serve and a good passing shot. Keep the return low to the server's feet and force him to volley up, giving you an easier passing shot. You can keep the ball low by hitting an overspin forehand or a "chip" backhand that takes some of the speed off the ball.

You must keep the ball in play at any cost to offset the initial offensive thrust of the serve and first volley. If you survive those two shots, the point will be turning in your favor. Serve and volley is exciting; just remember to take it in three stages—first serve, first volley and move in for the "kill."

All-court play

You might think of me as a serve and volley player. I follow my serve in to the net on most surfaces because I feel my first and second serves are strong enough to approach behind. Actually, I think of myself as an all-court player. I can play from the backcourt and work my way in to the net, if the conditions and my opponent make it necessary. Other all-court players include Rod Laver, Ken Rosewall and Jimmy Connors.

What distinguishes the all-court player is his ability to play well in the approach zone. This represents an advanced stage of development. In my own case, I don't think my basic ground strokes or volleys have changed much since I turned professional at the age of 23. The real improvement in my game since then has come in my ability and confidence to play shots in the approach zone.

The serve is not quite as important to most all-court players as it is to the serve and volley specialist; however, it must be a strong offensive weapon. Players using the all-court game must work constantly, moving rapidly from one zone to the next and exercising quick and rapid racquet head control. An ability to handle balls hit in the approach zone is how you can recognize the true talents of the all-court player. By improving this style, you can handle balls in the approach zone with more confidence and you can learn to move from offense

to defense with maximum flexibility.

A typical point might be to serve a wide slice to your opponent's forehand, causing him to hit a weak return to the middle of your court. You would then hit an approach shot down the line and move in to the net to volley his running backhand passing shot. If you reach the ball, you will have an easy volley to an open court for a winner.

It is tough to defend against an all-court player since he has a variety of shots in all zones at his disposal. However, you can test his preferences early in the match. For example, does he like a forehand or a backhand? Does he react better running side to side or up and back?

An interesting and basic rule of strategy is to play through an opponent's strength to get to his weakness. This can be very effective against a player who is completely controlling the match. For example, if a player has a strong forehand and a weak backhand, hit wide to his strong forehand. This will open the court and expose his weak backhand.

So you see there are basic styles of play that develop basic shots. The backcourt game develops your ground strokes; the serve and volley game develops your serve; and the all-court game develops your approach zone shots. Play all of them to improve your game. Pick out your favorite style and give it a good chance to work. If you are winning, never change it. If you are losing, always change it.

DOUBLES STRATEGY

Played properly and skillfully, doubles is more fun to play than singles. There is less court to cover and this brings me to the most important thing for you to remember about playing doubles—cover your half of the court.

58. STAY WITH YOUR PARTNER

In doubles play, both players should move up to the net together or play the backcourt together, in parallel formation to the net. This helps them to cover the whole court in the most effective way.

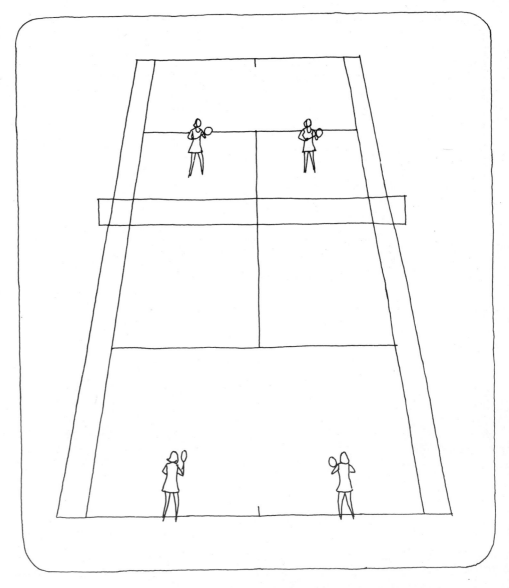

So many people stand near the alley when their partner is serving because they are afraid of being "sidelined." In reality, though, they are standing in a position where they can only cover one-third of the court; in effect, they are saying to their partner, "you cover two-thirds and I'll cover one-third." That is such an important point in doubles that I'll say it again: always position yourself so that you will have the best chance of covering your half of the court.

The two partners should move together in a formation parallel to the net (*see illustration #58*). Both players should be either up at the net together or at the baseline together. Avoid the "one-up-one-back" formation which leaves your team wide open to an easy volley from the opposing team's net man (*see illustration #59*). The objective is to gain

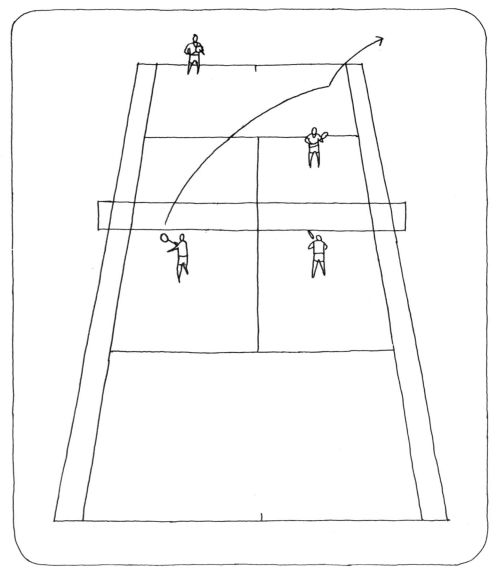

control of the net where you'll both be in a position to make simple shots to win the point.

Choosing a partner

Selection of a doubles partner is also important, especially if you have a club tournament or some other event coming up. The styles of play should be considered here; some people prefer to play the forehand court and some backhand. If you play forehand, then look for someone who prefers to play backhand.

The next thing to look for is someone you get along with, someone who is not a complainer. I feel that the pair who talks things over will have more success than the team who doesn't. You may need to change tactics as the match progresses. My regular partner, Tony Roche, and I often discuss tactics

60. BASIC DOUBLES

Basic doubles strategy is to serve to the receiver's backhand (A) and follow your serve to the volley position (dotted line). The receiver returns serve crosscourt (B) and then moves up (dotted line) to gain parallel position at the net with his or her partner. As the receiver moves up to the net (C), the server's first volley should be deep and down the middle. This allows him to get in parallel formation with his partner and gain a strong position at the net.

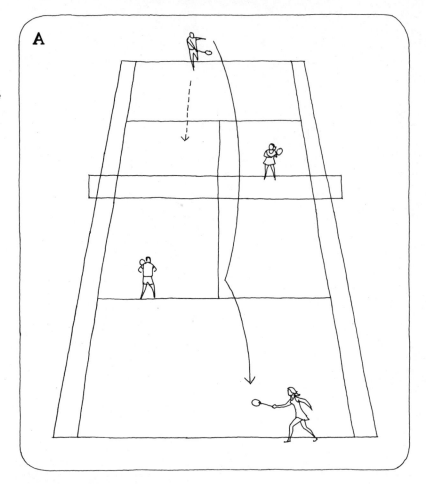

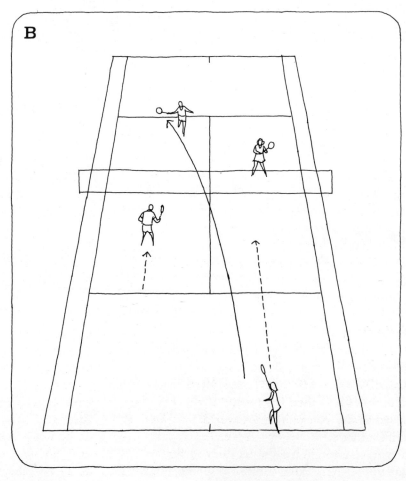

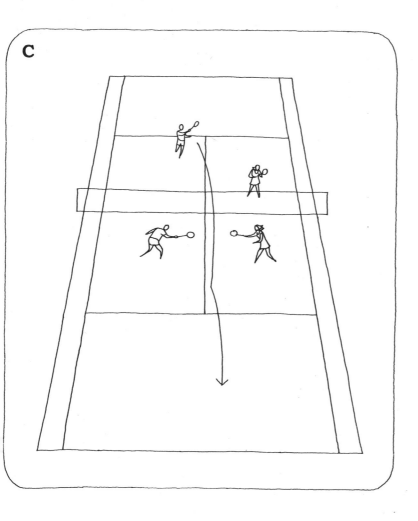

C

during a match, especially if we are losing.

What should you do when left-handers and right-handers mix in doubles? Normally, the left-hander should play on the left side of the court so that the team has both forehands covering the outside areas. This gives the team more range. Since you can stretch farther with your forehand than with your backhand, both players can cover more ground to the side and still stand close enough together to control the center.

A good doubles player is one who encourages his partner when his partner is having an off day, or praises him when he is playing well. It's important to have at least one player on the team who is steady. If both players run hot and cold, then your wins and losses will be erratic, too.

Get the first serve in

The first serve is really the secret of winning doubles. The pair that can get their first serves consistently in the court will more often than not come out on top. When Roche and I, who could be regarded as the best pair in the world, play against a team that gets a lot of first serves in the court, we usually have a tough match. As soon as our opponents begin missing their first serves, however,

we are able to play a good return and break quite easily.

The first serve should go in about 80 per cent of the time; take off some speed and add a little spin to give it more control. It should be directed mainly to the opponent's backhand (see *illustration #60A*). It is dangerous to serve the ball wide to the receiver's forehand, because that will allow him to open up the sideline of your partner.

The second serve should be hit with more spin; you should try to get it in as deep as possible so that you can follow it to the net. If you serve short, the receiver will be able to jump all over it and make a forceful return at your feet that causes you to miss the volley or play a weak shot.

After the serve is put into play, you should move to the net. The first volley should be hit as deep as possible into your opponent's court, after which you move into a closer net position ready for the putaway volley on the next shot (see *illustrations #60 B and C*). The first volley should never be hit from behind your service line; hit it from about three feet or more inside the service line, depending on how fast you can get there. If your first volley is deep and you and your partner are well-positioned at the net, there should be no way your opponents

61. DOUBLES POSITIONS

In doubles, the server should stand midway between the singles sideline and the center mark while his partner will be midway between the center line and the doubles sideline, 8 to 10 feet from the net. The receiver should stand close to the baseline near the alley and his partner should stand inside the service line between the center line and the singles sideline. Remember, you have the responsibility of covering your side of the court, both up and back.

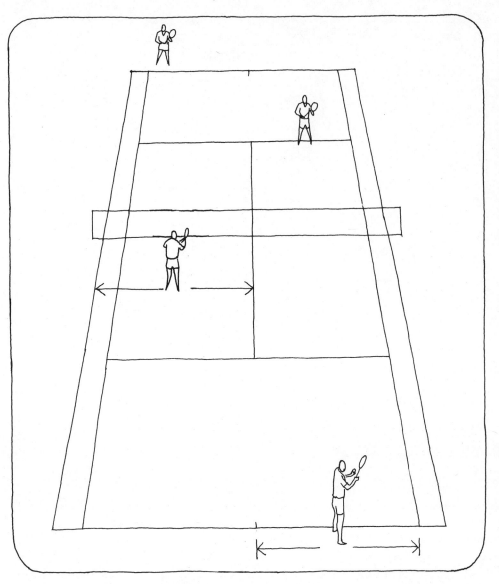

can make a passing shot. They will probably be forced to lob. If you find that you are having trouble with the receiver's return, then attempt to move to the net quicker so you can meet the volley higher.

I feel that children who are learning the game should not be forced too early to come to the net. But as soon as they are strong enough, they should be encouraged to practice their serve and volley game in doubles. If they can't serve and volley in doubles, then they have no chance of being able to serve and volley in singles.

Where to stand in doubles

The server should position himself approximately halfway between the center line and the singles sideline (*see illustration #61*). The server's partner (the net man) should stand halfway between the center line and the outside (doubles) sideline, and about 8 to 10 feet back from the net. Only a very tall person, like Stan Smith, can stand very close to

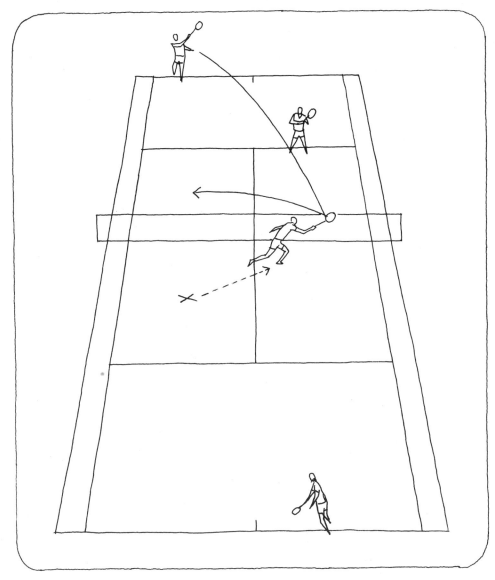

To poach, the server's partner moves over to cut off the service return with an angled volley. The server moves in to cover the half of the court vacated by the poacher. The poacher stays in his newly assumed position after hittting the volley.

the net, because he feels he can still run back, jump up and cover anything hit over his head. The position you want at the net is one where you feel comfortable in your ability to cover shots to your right, left, or over your head, in your half of the court.

The receiver should stand on or just behind the baseline, near the alley, which puts him in the best position to cover all possible angles in returning service. His partner should stand in the back of the service court, as shown in *illustration #61,* about halfway between the center line and the singles sideline. If the receiver returns low, passing the opposing net man, the receiver's partner can move up to the normal volleying position at the net. But if the return is high or goes to the other net man, the receiver's partner should retreat to cover the middle.

When your partner is serving, don't watch him. Keep your eyes on the receiver; out of the corner of your eye, watch the receiver's partner. As the receiver starts to take his backswing, watch his head closely. This will give you a good idea of where the return is coming and will enable you to anticipate his shot.

Poaching

Poaching, or trying to intercept the receiver's return, is a much discussed topic, especially in the United States. Poaching is when the net man crosses quickly along the net to cut off the return of service with a sharp volley (*see illustration #62*). Many club players are fond of poaching. I feel it is a little overdone.

The basic idea behind poaching is to upset the receiver's return and make him nervous so he'll push the ball instead of hitting freely. This usually pays off, but it can lead to trouble. There is nothing worse than moving across to intercept the return and have the receiver hit a winner straight down your sideline. The other difficulty when you are trying to poach comes when the receiver lobs the return of serve over your head. You are so committed and intent on moving to your right or left, that you are not looking for the lob.

The server and his partner should agree when they will try a poach. Often the net man senses when the moment is right and signals his partner, the server, behind his back. When your team decides to poach, the server should serve very deep. As soon as the receiver hits the ball, the net man moves rapidly across to his partner's side of the court hoping to meet the receiver's crosscourt return and volley it away.

At the same time, the server, instead of going directly to the net, a position now occupied by his poaching partner, moves up quickly to the other side of the court to cover the half vacated by the poacher.

Roche and I rarely poach when the other is serving, but we are always ready to jump on the ball hit lazily toward the middle of the court. A good partnership is one where the partners move with the ball and with each other. You shouldn't poach unless you are pretty sure of putting away the volley because you are exposing your team to a delicate situation.

When you are playing with a partner who stays on the baseline after serving, you should keep your net position, unless you feel your partner is in trouble. You will know he is in trouble if the receiver and his or her partner both move to the net position. Then your partner should lob and you should retreat as quickly as possible to the baseline and take a position there with your partner. If the two of you are at the net and a lob goes over one player's head, it is his job to either smash or run after that ball. This goes back to the basic doubles principle I talked about, to cover your half of the court.

The exception is when one person is at net and the other is back, and a lob goes over the net player's head. In that case, the partner playing back may run across and take the ball; the net person will cross to cover the other side, and either stay in the net position or move back to the baseline.

Players in the beginner and intermediate stage probably feel more comfortable playing from the baseline. This is wrong thinking, because this is only defensive tennis. You will never learn to play offensive tennis unless you practice playing at the net. When you limit yourself to playing from the baseline only, you are playing only half the game.

Receiver

In doubles, place yourself in a position to receive serve near the sideline. This will reduce the possibility of the server scoring an angle ace. To return the first serve, you should be in a position on or just behind the baseline, depending on your ability to control the speed of serve. For the second serve, move inside the baseline.

If the server comes to the net, hit the return as low as possible so the server will volley up and set up your next shot. If the server stays back, try to keep the ball away from the net man, and return the ball deep to the server.

If, after you hit a deep return, the server returns a short ball, play an approach shot and move to the net. But, if he volleys to your forehand at about three-quarter court depth, you have several options —a down-the-line passing shot, a shot down the center or an offensive lob.

A basic principle of doubles play is, when in doubt, play the ball low and down the middle of the court. The reason is that this limits your opponents' angle and makes it difficult for them to hit a winner off this shot.

If the server volleys deep, my chances of making a passing shot are very small. So, I often elect to hit a high lob to get our team back into the rally. One of my favorite tactics, after I have used the lob several times, is to whip over a low crosscourt passing shot. I can only get away with this tactic once or twice in a match, but it is worthwhile saving for the right occasion.

A good shot off a short volley is a soft dink shot at the net man's feet. This is hit with a short backswing and with just enough speed to carry it low over the net straight at the net man. He will have no option but to volley it back to you.

What should the receiver do when the net man is poaching on him? When I am playing against someone I know likes to poach, the answer is to hit the ball straight down the line. Poachers usually like to stand very close to the net, so hit the ball hard and low, straight at them. Whether they are in motion or

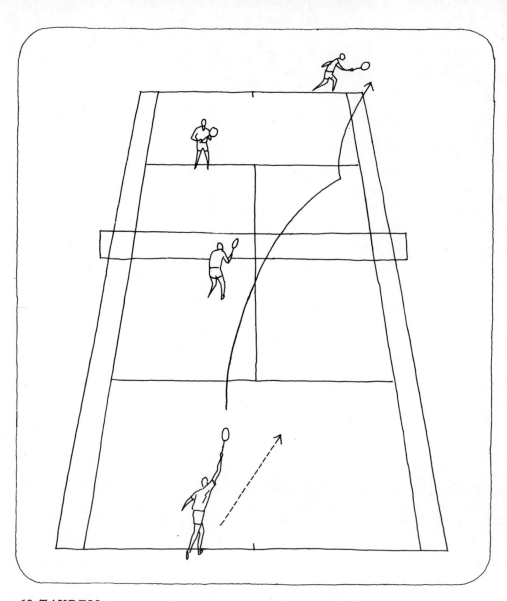

63. TANDEM FORMATION

In the Australian, or tandem, formation, the server's partner stands on the same half of the court as the server to cut off the expected cross-court return. It's a useful way of confusing your opponents and changing a losing game.

not, it is very hard for them to volley the ball away.

One more shot to have up your sleeve in returning serve is the lob over the net man. Even if it doesn't go for a winner, it makes the net man a little wary of poaching.

Receiver's partner

When your partner is receiving serve, don't watch him. Keep your eye on the server as he or she moves to the net; out of the corner of your eye, watch the net person to see your opponents cross, or poach. If the return is low, then move a little right to left, or left to right, to make the server watch you instead of the ball.

Advanced players might want to try a little bit of fun in experimenting with two systems. One is called "scissors" and the other is "tandem." Scissors is played when your team is serving and you have a prior arrangement whereby, as soon as the serve goes into court, the net person crosses over to the other side and the server runs in and takes the net man's original position. The basic idea of this is to try to upset the receiving team and make them miss the return of serve.

Tandem is when the net man lines up on the same side of the court as the server (see *illustration #63*). This is sometimes called the "Australian" formation. It discourages a crosscourt return; the server then runs to the other side of the court to cover a down-the-line return.

In doubles, four people should be in motion once the server puts the ball in play. You should never stand on your heels when the ball is in motion.

I have personally stood beside the court at my tennis ranch and yelled at students to keep on their toes. Their movement and doubles game improves immediately.

MIXED DOUBLES STRATEGIES

The basic doubles strategies I've described also apply to mixed doubles. The only difference between the two games is the difference between the relative strength and weakness of the partners. While men are not always stronger partners than women, I think that in most mixed doubles pairings the man is the stronger of the two. Your strategy for mixed doubles should reflect this.

The stronger player will always move to cover more of the court, a situation that is fairly common in mixed doubles. If you have a very weak partner, you would expect to cover as much as two-thirds of the court.

For example, when a woman partner comes to the net she should assume a position closer to the net than normally recommended for doubles— about five feet from it. This will allow her to put away volleys more easily. However, this leaves her exposed to the lob, and here the man must cover for her.

Playing mixed doubles with my wife in club tournaments is the most difficult thing I have ever tried. The first year we were married, Angie and I played mixed doubles together. I wanted to win badly for Angie's sake, and quite often would try so hard that my game deteriorated. This made me mad and I would start cursing and throwing my racquet. Angie would then abuse me because she said I was not enjoying playing with her. The next

time we played together, I decided to give it the "casual" treatment, hoping that I would play better and not get so mad. She would abuse me once again, for not caring if we won or lost. After one year of this, I said, "That's the last time we are playing mixed doubles in a tournament together."

We love to play social tennis together because we have fun, but tournament tennis doesn't seem to work out for us or for most other married couples we know. If any of you have a solution to this, I wish you'd drop me a note and tell me about it.

Personally, I feel that the whole point of social mixed doubles is for all four players to enjoy the match and themselves.

In doubles it's easy to overcome differences in playing abilities. One partner can help out his teammate if she's weak in some strokes. The stronger player can make the weak player better than she is, by encouraging her and controlling the play in such a way that she will have easier shots in good position. He can coach her on what to expect, so that she won't have to struggle to keep up with the others. The weak player's aims should be to be as consistent as possible and play good position.

If you can approach mixed doubles with this attitude, I think you'll get a lot more pleasure from playing together.

PLAYING THE ELEMENTS

Make the elements of wind and sun work for you rather than against you. That's part of strategy for both singles and doubles. The loser may complain that the wind or the sun made play very difficult. The winner rarely says that. I have to admit that I

don't mind playing on a windy day because I use the wind to help me. You can do the same.

Playing in the wind

The wind will affect your shots more if you are playing from the baseline rather than at the net.

If the wind is behind you, take the ball early because the wind will be holding the ball away from you. The same wind will cause your shots to carry deeper, so aim a little lower over the net. If you normally aim about three feet over the net, make it about two feet now. You might also put some topspin on the ball to make it drop a little faster into your opponent's court.

Although your volleying will be little affected by the wind, be on the lookout for an offensive lob. Your opponent will be able to hit a hard, low lob over your head and use the wind to keep the ball in court.

When you're serving with the wind behind you, don't toss too high or the wind will blow the ball forward. Add a little more spin to your serve to make sure that it has more control.

Playing against the wind, conditions are reversed. It will cause your shots to be pulled down in your opponent's court. Thus, your ground strokes should be hit higher over the net so that they will go deep into the other court. Spin will not be necessary, so you can hit the ball flatter—and higher.

Serving against the wind, you can take off some spin and hit it a little flatter to make sure that it doesn't drop too soon and give your opponent an easy return.

If the wind is gusting, particularly crosscourt, it's

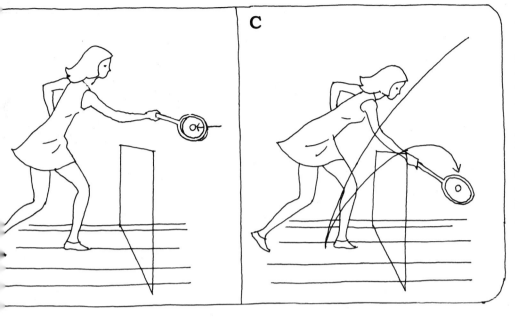

tough to make the wind work for you. In that case, the only thing to do is to play with caution. Take advantage of the easy shots and don't take unnecessary risks. A few modifications to your game, as I've suggested, will allow you to be more effective in the wind.

Playing into the sun

The sun can be a particularly difficult element to deal with. At midday, it's hard to look up for a serve or an overhead, and late in the day the sun can cast annoying shadows which cause you to lose sight of the ball.

If you find that the sun is in your line of vision when you're serving or hitting overheads, try to adjust your position so that you are out of the sun's glare but still able to keep your eyes on the ball. It may help to change the position of your toss slightly.

If your eyes are sensitive to strong sunlight, I'd advise that you wear a cap or a visor. Sunglasses may help although they do restrict your vision to some extent. Remember that you should change sides every other game so your opponent will get his share of the annoying sun, too.

RULES THAT WILL HELP YOU WIN

If you're going to get the most out of your tennis strategies, you owe it to yourself to learn the rules of the game. You can get a copy of the rules at most tennis shops or by writing the United States Tennis Association in Princeton, N.J. Just knowing the rules can help you win points.

For example, you may not reach over the net to

65. HITTING AROUND THE NET
A ball hit outside the net post and into the opposing court is a good return even if it passes at a height lower than the net.

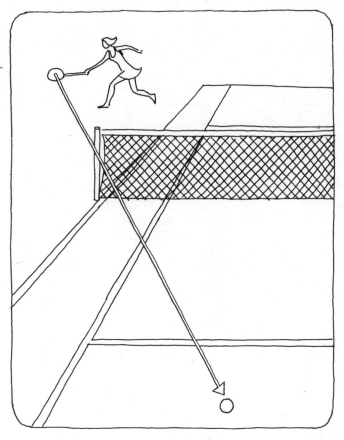

contact a ball. The exception to this rule is if the ball hits on your side of the court and bounces back across the net. You may then reach out across the net, without touching it, to contact the ball (*see illustration #64C*). Your racquet may, however, cross the net so long as you have actually hit the ball on your side of the net and your racquet is in the act of following through (*see illustration #64A.*)

You should also learn the "ball in play" section of the rules. For example, if you are driven far out of the side of the court so that your return doesn't actually pass over the net, that is considered a legal shot. In fact, the ball can actually pass the net post at a height lower than the net (*see illustration #65*) so long as your return hits in the court.

Although it rarely happens in a match, if a loose ball is lying on the court and the ball you are playing strikes it, the ball is still alive (*see illustration #66*).

A very common infringement of the "ball in play" rules is catching a ball on the fly, especially one that your opponent has hit far out of court (*see illustration #67C*). This ball is still alive and the point goes to your opponent. A less common situation arises if the server in doubles hits the opposing net man by mistake before the ball has touched the court. It would take a pretty wild serve to do this but, alas for the receiving team, this is a point for the server (*see illustration #67A*).

These are just a few examples of how a knowledge of the rules can help you win.

THE WILL TO WIN
A knowledge of strategy plus an ability to stroke the ball correctly are, of course, the basic ingredients of a successful tennis game. But there's one other element we can't forget and that's desire, the will to win. The player who hustles, who goes for every ball, who never lets up on himself or his opponent, is going to win more than his or her share of matches. On the international tennis circuit, there isn't that much difference technically among players. They all know how and where to hit the ball. It's the ones who force themselves to concentrate harder and try harder who get to the top in the game and stay there year after year.

The number one fault I see in my junior players is the tendency not to give credit to an opponent for forcing them into an error. Too often I hear "I can't believe I missed that" or "He's so lucky" or "Sure" or "I'm so unlucky" or similar fruitless outbursts. Some adults also fall into this category. I was taught to show or say nothing that would give my opponent the impression that I might be frightened to lose.

So while you may have all the tools to win, they count for relatively little if you don't also have the will to win.

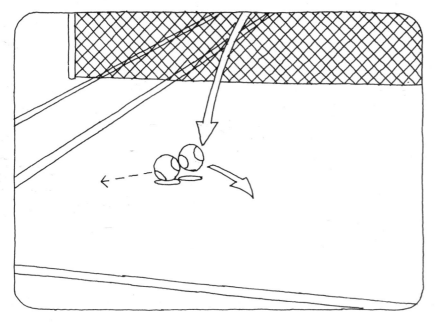

66. KEEP COURT CLEAR OF LOOSE BALLS

When the ball in play strikes another ball lying in the court, the ball is still in play and play must continue. It's up to the players to keep their courts free of loose balls.

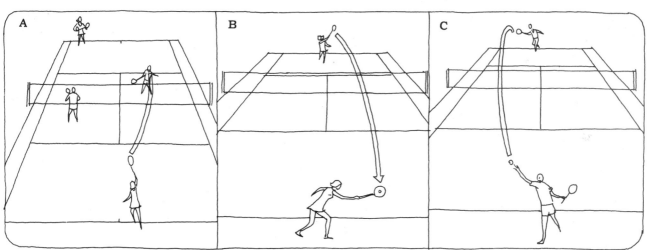

A   B   C

67. BALL-IN-PLAY RULES

You will lose the point if a ball in play touches any part of you, even if you are hit by a serve (A). You will also lose the point if your racquet "catches" or stops a ball that is clearly going out of court (B) or if you catch a ball that has not yet bounced (C).

GREAT ALL-COURT, SERVE AND VOLLEY, AND BACKCOURT PLAYERS

An all-court game is essential for consistent performance on all surfaces. This is my basic and preferred style. I like to control the ball from the backcourt, attack the ball in the approach zone and put the ball away in the volleying area. On a slow court I am forced to be more patient and to play more from the backcourt, building my position to the net. There are two other basic styles of play—the backcourt player, like Chris Evert (above right) or Bjorn Borg, who rely mostly on maneuvering their opponents with ground strokes from the back of the court; and the serve-and-volley player, like Arthur Ashe (above left), or Stan Smith, who rely mostly on a big serve and a quick volley at the net for winners. Here I am, at left, playing on grass and trying to attack at every opportunity. However, I must develop a good defense to counter my opponent's offense.

POACHING

Signals can sometimes confuse your opponents. In the top photo my partner Tarzan (Ron Ely), at left, is signalling he is going to cross to his right after I serve. He does and I move up quickly (at right) to cover his side; just as well, because my opponent has guessed right!

ANTICIPATION

Anticipation is a big part of your strategy. In the photo left, my partner is very close to the net and I am anticipating a lob over his head. I will call out "Mine," and he should cross to my side. In doubles (see photo above) you should divide the court into two halves. Each partner is responsible for covering his side of the court, up and back. In this picture, Tony Roche is on his way to the net to get in the parallel formation with his partner, wife Sue. The team that gets to the net first in doubles will have the advantage.

CHAPTER 6: THE FAMILY GAME

I was luckier than a lot of youngsters starting out in tennis. My whole family played. My mother and my father, who was a dentist, played social tennis. My older sister played tennis on a club level and, when I was old enough, I began the game, too. Then my younger sister followed in our footsteps.

So the whole family was involved in tennis, and it's a pleasure for me to look back now and remember how all of us played together, practiced together, competed together and had fun together despite our varying abilities. There was constant laughter, lots of good natured teasing, serious games and not-so-serious games. Sometimes we were plain awful, and sometimes we were spectacular. It didn't matter, though. We were a real unit, and it was tennis that brought us together. We all enjoyed it—and each other—tremendously.

You never know where a solid tennis background will lead you. In my case, of course, the game became a full-time career. With my sisters, it became an enjoyable way to have fun and relax. The great thing about it, though, is that once you've learned tennis, it will stay with you for the rest of your life.

PRACTICING TOGETHER

Family participation in tennis, I believe, should be built around practice sessions or rallies together. That not only brings everybody together, it also gives each member an opportunity to practice—and learn—by hitting tennis balls. Where else can you find people willing to trade shots for an hour or more and for free? No matter how much better—or worse—he may be, Father can improve by hitting with Mother, Mother can benefit from hitting with her son, Father with his daughter and so on, because repetition, if done properly, is what counts.

A word of caution, however, right at the start: though Father may be the best player and feels, as a result, that he should become the family teacher, he should approach this role very carefully. I've found it's terribly difficult for a man to teach his wife, or vice-versa, a practical skill, whether it's tennis, how to drive a car, or what have you. And it's difficult for a parent to teach a child, too. For one thing, the adult is probably not qualified to do it anyway. And the process can often only aggravate normal family tensions. The better the player, the less he says and the more he rallies.

What I prefer to see when a family practices together is that teaching and learning be restricted to hitting balls to each other (to weak spots preferably) or to feeding balls to each other in practice drills. An experienced father, for instance, should concentrate on directing balls to the spot where he knows his son or daughter needs practice. He shouldn't allow much conversation because that can be distracting and turn what should be just a player-player relationship into a father-daughter or father-son relationship. A family should definitely practice together, but they should be very wary about instructing each other.

KEEP IT FUN

Always remember that tennis is a *game* and that the emphasis should be on making it fun for every member of the family. Parents should be careful that they don't expect too much of their children on the court—or husbands of wives, for that matter.

Each person in a family should be treated individually on court. His or her abilities, size, needs and goals should be kept in mind at all times. For example, I think it's wise for parents to take a good objective look at a child and try to project the type of person he or she is going to be. Then, they should design a style of play that matches the child's characteristics. But if a child has been playing a while, parents should not attempt to change his or her playing style. Leave that to the judgment of a teaching professional.

Progress can be monitored, of course, but always in view of a youngster's ability, interest and available time. A junior who's playing twice a week obviously shouldn't be expected to improve at the same rate as one who's playing five times a week. They're on two different programs and should have two different sets of goals. The important thing is that the family create an environment where each member can improve to the best of his ability.

One thing a parent can contribute to that environment is a sense of sportsmanship. That should be stressed from the beginning. A youngster who misbehaves on court not only reveals something about himself, he's also saying something about his upbringing. When I play sets with my family, I try to hit the ball to where they can handle it most comfortably and I make sure the score ends up close. But I give them the benefit of the doubt on balls that land close to the line. I don't cheat on calls. Children copy their parents' behavior.

HANDICAPPING

Even if members of a family play on different levels, it's possible for them to play sets against each other by using a handicap system. It's not that easy in tennis to handicap players, but it can be done. For instance, you can give the better player a smaller area to hit into and the weaker one a larger area. In other words, if I'm better than you are, I'll play the singles court while you'll have the entire doubles court to aim at. We could cut it down even more than that. I would use just one half of the singles court, while you would use both sides. Another handicap method is to let the weaker player serve from a position closer to the net, say, from the service line. Or the stronger player can be allowed just one, instead of two serves.

The best handicap formula I've found is a point system which gives the weaker player the lead at the start of a game or set. He can be awarded a 30-love advantage for each game, say, or a two-love lead in games for each set. A few games will indicate how much of a handicap will even things up. The great thing about this system is that you can have a close match almost every time and still play to your own standards.

IMPROVEMENT

A family will get the most out of tennis, and enjoy it more, if everyone is able to improve his or her game at a reasonable rate. One way to help that process along is a family tennis calendar. Map out a two-week program which specifies what each member of the family will do over that period. Write down the days Mother will be playing, Father will be playing and the children will be playing. Then, assign a program to each. Set aside time for lessons, practice, matches and, if your family is ready for it, a family tournament. Two weeks is a good period because if it rains for a day or two,

it won't wash your program out completely. The whole idea of a family program, especially for beginning families, is to get into a tennis routine and then make it a habit.

You needn't neglect your friends, however. Playing with the same people all the time can be dull. Break the routine once in a while by playing somebody new. One of the nice things about tennis —for youngsters, housewives, businessmen and even touring pros—is the opportunity it offers to meet new friends and new tennis partners. You add to your circle of court acquaintances every time you play in a tournament.

There are many tennis clinics and camps that offer players of every level concentrated doses of tennis designed to help them improve quickly. Once a family, or an individual, has become involved in the game, a week or two at a tennis camp can be the fastest way to progress—and you'll have fun while you're at it. The best part of some tennis camps is that a family can remain together while each member pursues individual goals.

WHERE TO PLAY

As more and more families take up tennis, the problem many of them have is finding a court where they can play the game. The industry can't seem to build tennis courts fast enough to keep up with the demand. Where to play, then, is usually the initial step any family starting out has to take —and it may be the most difficult step of all.

The first thing a family should do is look around its neighborhood for a court. There are municipal courts in most cities now and nearly all schools have tennis courts. You usually have to check the times they are available. Look around and see where the action is. Normally you'll find a tennis program at the municipal center; that's the hub of most tennis activity. Or, if you can afford it, look into the local tennis clubs. A tennis club will offer tennis programs for every member of the family as well as teaching professionals who are qualified to conduct the programs. Each club has a personality all its own; it's an expression of the man who's running it and of the people who are in it. I would definitely advise families to visit a club personally before joining. Most clubs will allow you to come in as a guest or just to visit.

Wherever you look, check the caliber of tennis. Does the club have only top players or does it have some beginners, too? Are there enough players on your family's level to meet your standards and needs? Then look over the facility itself. Is there a teaching professional on hand? What about the programs offered? Is it a club that makes juniors sit on the sidelines when an adult wants to play or does it encourage young players? For a family situation, you want to have one that encourages the younger members. If you find a father and son or mother and daughter playing, that's a good sign. Are there leagues? Is there a ladder? (A tennis ladder is a numbered list of players who try to advance upward by challenging players listed above them or turn back challenges from players listed below them.) Can you show up almost anytime without a reservation and have a good chance of getting a court? Are there enough courts to accommodate all of the family so you won't spend much time waiting? Of course, the final consideration is the financial one. Can you afford the cost for an entire family?

But whatever you do, get started. Once you've done that, you're bound to meet others who know the local tennis scene and can advise you further.

TAKING LESSONS

The best way for children to start out in the game is by taking group lessons—while the family helps them practice what they learn. Children like to be around other children when learning. When I was four, for instance, I would hit the ball around with my family whenever they played. When they saw I was hitting the ball over the net with regularity (I was about six then) and that I had a good eye and liked to play, they sent me to a Saturday morning tennis school. There were others like me around and it was fun for me to go there. It wasn't a chore. Only when I was 10 did I start taking private lessons.

Parents shouldn't push their kids into tennis lessons. If they want to play tennis, they will, without too much help from Mother and Father. What parents should do is expose their children to the game and see if they develop an interest in playing. Some children, of course, may not want to learn because they're shy or may not have too much ball sense. They feel they might be embarrassed because other youngsters can hit the ball back and they can't. That kind of child should be encouraged—but not forced—to learn how to play. Once he or she knows how, an interest might develop that will last a lifetime.

Anyone starting out in the game should take group lessons first before going on to private ones. For one thing, it's more economical. Second, you automatically meet a group of people you can play with between lessons, which means you're not lacking for practice partners. And, three, you can probably accomplish more in the relaxed atmosphere of group lessons than you can individually. Private lessons are important, too—I'm not saying they aren't—but only when you're advanced a bit or when you might be having a difficult time keeping up with the group.

When people take group instruction and watch five or six other people serving or hitting forehands, they develop a pretty thorough understanding of that stroke; much more so than they do by just watching videotapes of their own shot. When someone sees six other forehands and then his own, he knows a lot better what he's going to have to do.

Here's another advantage to group instruction: in tennis, you're always running into different styles of players. When you're part of a group, you are introduced to different styles and you become familiar with them. Then when you go out to play, there won't be so many surprises. Your next opponent might even be one of your former classmates.

When you decide to take lessons, what do you look for in a teaching pro? I wouldn't like to send Clint to someone else to be coached without checking out the pro first. Above all, I'd want to be sure that the lessons would be conducted in a relaxed, not regimented, way. It has to be fun to practice, fun to learn and fun to play tennis. The best teaching pro is one who's obviously well trained in the basics, greets progress with enthusiasm and creates an atmosphere that induces laughter and relaxation.

One word of caution: don't rush out and enter the first tournament you can after taking a lesson. Practice for a couple of weeks and try to incorporate into your game what you've been taught. That's the only way to get the most out of your lessons and really improve.

Say you go to a pro for a half-hour lesson. Waiting on the next court is your friend Fred, who's hoping you'll get finished with your lesson so he can play you. But don't oblige Fred by running right over to play him after your lesson. He may start beating you, and you may be tempted to revert to what you were doing before the lesson. You'll forget the lesson completely. "Gee, I beat Fred last week," you'll say to yourself, "so I've got to start doing what I was doing then." The lesson, at that point, will be forgotten—and wasted. There's only one way to do it right and that is to hit lots and lots of balls until the lesson has become ingrained.

EQUIPMENT

Every tennis family should be sure that it's properly equipped for the game. There's more to this than meets the eye, with so many kinds of racquets, balls, shoes, socks, shorts, shirts, dresses, accessories, colors, sweat bands, hats and so on to consider. Everybody in the family has different needs, too, so it's best not to rush into a mass buying spree.

Many beginning players ask me which they should get—a metal or a wood racquet. A metal racquet will probably produce more power, but it's a little more difficult to control. The ball leaves a metal frame with a little more force. The wooden racquet, I feel, gives the beginner a little more control of the ball with probably less power. My suggestion is to purchase your racquet where you'll get the best advice, either at a sporting goods store which has a specialist on racquets or from a pro or coach who is qualified to select the proper racquet for your type of play.

The weight of the racquet is more important than whether it's made of metal or wood. If you get a metal racquet, try a lighter model than you would get in wood; that's because you won't need the extra weight for power. Too many players use too much tennis racquet; that is, they get ones that are too heavy and that they can't control the way they should. This can be a real handicap, especially for youngsters and weaker players.

Women players may be happier with metal racquets since they get a little more flexibility out of them—as well as more power, which they need. As for boys or girls, I prefer to start them with wooden racquets in a size that fits their physical builds. Youngsters who don't have their own racquets usually pick up their mother's or father's and think they can start right in with that. It's not a good idea.

Beginners from 8 to 10 years old should use junior racquets, two inches shorter than usual, with a grip size running from 4 to $4\frac{1}{2}$ inches in circumference. An average woman's would be light, with a grip running from $4\frac{3}{8}$ to $4\frac{1}{2}$, while an average man's would be heavier with a grip size starting at $4\frac{5}{8}$, medium weight.

Racquets can be strung with either nylon or gut. Nylon will work all right for a beginner. He won't have to worry about the humidity affecting it or the strings snapping in the rain. He would have to worry about that kind of thing if he used gut.

When gut gets wet, it expands and the coils can unravel. Since it's a woven material, it will break. It can be patched, but that's a bother. Synthetic strings are improving all the time, but the better players are still playing with gut, which bites and holds onto the ball better than nylon.

If you can afford it, it's a good idea to have two racquets—identical ones, at that. With two identical racquets, you can alternate them as you play. This way, you'll get longer wear out of a pair than you would buying one at a time. Two racquets, alternated in use, last twice as long because you're giving one of them a rest half of the time.

Next to the racquet, your tennis shoes are your most critical piece of equipment. Blisters will put you out of business quicker than anything else. Every member of the family should be outfitted with well-made regulation tennis shoes. Avoid getting the inexpensive ones that won't give you the support you need. There are two basic kinds: the leather shoe and the canvas shoe, and I have no preference between them. The better grade of either will give excellent support. You should also look for good traction in the sole. Some persons may think tennis shoes feel awfully heavy, but they're really not. It just appears that way because they have better soles with more foundation to them.

If you're playing on a hard court, it's extremely important not only to find a proper tennis shoe, but also to wear two pairs of socks, a light pair with the regular athletic sock on top. This allows a sock to slide on a sock instead of a sock to slide on a foot, which causes a blister.

No matter what the temperature, you should always have a light sweater or jacket to put on immediately after playing to cool down muscles. This will help to eliminate aching muscles or tennis elbow. Most top players prefer to warm up in a jacket or sweater because it helps them warm up a little quicker.

As for tennis shorts, shirts and dresses, don't forget that there is a fall line, a spring line and a summer line for each. For instance, a good cotton shirt, or one made of polyester and cotton, absorbs perspiration and can keep you cool on a hot day. Very dark colors may make you too warm, which is why you still see a lot of white shirts or pastels in the summertime. Men can wear a mesh-type shirt or a sun shirt, which "breathes" more than the other kind. But women's clothes have even more varied styles, depending on the season. There are different fabrics and fashions for winter and summer play.

Court attire depends a lot on personal preference. It should always offer freedom of movement. Try your tennis clothes on before buying them to make sure they move with your different stretching motions. Some hang in such a way that when you go up for a ball, your shirttail goes out and stays out. If you stretch for a wide shot, your dress should rise with you. A test is necessary before buying to learn if the material rides with your shoulder in the serving and overhead motions, for example.

CONDITIONING

To obtain any kind of consistency in tennis, you have to be in good condition. Not everyone should follow the same conditioning program, however. Conditioning the body is different for the tournament player than it is for the office worker who plays mostly on his lunch hour. Conditioning is different for the mother who needs exercise as opposed to most children, who usually get plenty.

It will always be a problem for the man who goes from an air-conditioned office to an air-conditioned automobile and then walks onto a court that's blazing under 80- or 90-degree heat. If his body lacks a certain degree of fitness, this kind of abuse just serves to break it down.

Those on erratic schedules should try to keep up a consistent exercise program, making sure to take a good warm-up before going out on the court. Just doing a few minutes a day of simple calisthenics and stretching exercises will help a great deal. I feel that a lot of the aches and pains, tennis elbows and pulled leg muscles are simply the result of making a switch from cold to heat a little too quickly.

I went to a gym when I was 11 or 12. I believed in keeping my body in good condition even then. Today at my tennis camp in Texas, I find that whole families are sore and stiff after the first day of simple exercises. It proves to me that not enough people prepare themselves properly for any kind of physical activity. For a family, I suggest running, simple stomach exercises, push-ups to develop the shoulders and arms, sit-ups to strengthen the mid-section and leg bends to build up leg muscles. Rotating, jumping, stretching and running exercises seem to be the most effective.

The important thing is to be consistent. When you miss a day or two of tennis, go through some exercises. Then use the game of tennis itself as a conditioner. It's best, however, not to force anyone in the family to exercise. You can talk about its value and set a good example yourself, but it's not good to force anyone to exercise.

Skipping rope is very good because it involves all of the muscular activities that are used in tennis —control, endurance, speed, coordination, strength and relaxation. This is probably the best general exercise for tennis players of all levels.

For the keener members of the family, distance running at some stage in the year is a good way to build up endurance. A mile, two miles or five miles of jogging on a regular schedule has a two-fold purpose: 1) it gives a certain amount of long-term wind; and 2) it teaches self-discipline by making you go out on a regular basis and do something which is not all that much fun.

PRACTICE

Any good conditioning program should involve practicing tennis. If you can make your body more physically fit, and improve your tennis at the same time, what could be better? Drills on the court are one effective method. If you can, find someone to keep you constantly moving by hitting balls at you for five minutes at a time or by making you run and stretch as well as practice shots. Hitting balls while you're winded, which is what happens in a real match, is one of the best drills I know of for any player.

The number of balls you hit in practice has a great deal to do with how effective the practice is. If you can't find someone to rally with you, the next best thing is a ball machine; most clubs and teaching pros have one. A bucket of balls is a necessity, too. You don't want just a can or two. What you need in practice is to hit and hit and hit, over and over and over, knowing there's always another ball coming at you.

You can improve your game by probably 20 per cent just by concentrating on a single problem area. Let's say it's the return of service. A two-week period should be devoted to just improving the return of service. If you give yourself a day or two only, then you'll lose out. You'll have one good day on the court, but then you'll probably miss the next day because of rain or a business appointment. That's the way life goes, so you should prepare for it.

Personally, I like to practice when nobody else is around. I go to the court where I have a back-board. I give myself a two-week program on that backboard. I don't walk out and hit against the backboard and hope that somebody comes along. Even Clint hits against the wall a lot. I didn't tell him to, either. I just said, "When I was young I used to hit against a wall all the time." Then I walked away. The next thing I knew, he was hitting the ball against the wall.

The way you use a backboard or wall can help or hurt your game. The danger is that by hitting the ball too hard you'll develop unnatural strokes. That's because the harder you hit the ball against the wall, the quicker it comes back. Stand back from the wall farther than normal and take the ball on the second, not the first bounce. This will more closely duplicate the speed with which the ball comes back to you on court.

Use the backboard to a purpose. For example, you can draw a line across the wall at net height, and another line three feet above that. That will give you practice in hitting shots that clear the net by three feet. Or draw square targets on the wall, one in the center and one to the side of that (see *illustration #68*). When you aim for the center box, you'll get practice hitting crosscourt shots; when you aim for the box on the side, it will give you practice hitting shots down the line.

When you have another player to practice with, so much the better. It doesn't matter if you're not equal in ability, either. For instance, here's how to practice with a weaker player.

Say you, as a mother, want to practice a running forehand and your young daughter wants to practice, too. Put her at about mid-court. Let her drop the ball and stroke it to the center of your court. As you return that, she hits a second shot away from you, which makes you hit that ball on the run. The weaker player is not expected to get the ball back or even chase it but simply acts as a feeder, dropping ball after ball and hitting them at you. She's a ball machine you can talk with. But this drill also gives the weaker player some valuable

practice in hitting the ball from a bounce position. So you've accomplished two things: practice for your daughter in hitting a bouncing ball and for you in returning a running forehand. Both of you are getting improvement out of one practice session despite the difference in your levels of play.

Always try to simulate actual playing conditions in practice when you can. A player should not hit a ball and then move to an area where a shot would not normally be returned. Plan a sequence of shots with your practice partner. There are all sorts of variations on this theme. One might be a serve by Daughter, a return of serve by Mother, a lob by Daughter and an overhead by Mother. This gives both of you practice on specific strokes. That's when practice leads to improvement.

More advanced players can start with a serve, make a return of serve to an agreed-upon spot and then play the rest of the point all the way through. They'll plan during the rally to hit a forehand, a backhand, a short forehand and a volley to each other. Later, they'll add more variations. Practice for them becomes a progression of drills designed to place the ball where improvement is needed.

When there is an odd number of players for practice—three, for instance—you can have two-on-one practice. One player is at the net working on volleys while the other two play back at the baseline in their court hitting ground strokes to the net man. Then, change around.

68. DRILLS FOR THE BACKBOARD

A good backboard practice drill is to mount or draw two targets about three feet above the net line to represent shots down the line and crosscourt. To practice your crosscourt shots, hit to the center target. To practice down-the-line shots, hit to the target on the right.

When you practice, try to remember these four points: 1) practice must have repetition; 2) practice should have simulated playing conditions; 3) practice should duplicate actual playing pressure; 4) practice should be a pleasure.

You have to *want* to be a player before you become one.

WARMING UP

One phase of the game that doesn't get enough attention with some families is the warm-up. Some women practice too much before playing, leaving themselves too little time to play, while some men start a game right away and don't warm up enough. There are several ways to warm up and still have a lot of fun.

The first thing players should do as they walk out on the court is to turn off mentally as much as they can the daily cares of the office, the car pool or the load of homework. They should start putting themselves into a playing frame of mind.

When I go out to play after laying off for awhile, I like to get the feel of the racquet on the way to the court or practice area. I'll take the racquet in my hand, feel the forehand and backhand grips and go through a couple of phantom swings without hitting the ball just to get the timing of the racquet moving with my weight.

The purpose of the warm-up is to get the muscles warmed up, the feet moving and reacting to the ball, and the racquet head under control. Once I get in position for the warm-up, my first objective is to get the ball on the strings in the center of the racquet. I don't hit too hard, but try to make certain I am

moving properly through those three basic stages: the preparation, the hitting zone and the finish.

After I get the feel of the racquet head and get used to the ball's bounce, I then work on my movement. I try to take at least three small steps before I hit the ball, even if I don't have to run for it. That helps me to get moving and to get moving rapidly. Then I hit a good number of volleys, not to put them away, but just to control the ball off my racquet. As I move back, I start using a fuller swing —one with more backswing and follow-through. Then I take some overheads and serves. Most important, though, I try to stay relaxed. And all through my warm-up, I practice watching the ball.

If a person hasn't been playing much, he should not force an extra long warm-up on his opponent, who wants to play sooner. He should take some time before he goes to the court to hit the ball against a wall or to warm up some other way beforehand. When you play on courts where court-time is expensive, a long practice warm-up can run into money, too.

On a cold day you'll find it takes longer to get moving. Just be sure you spend enough time on your serves and your movement so that you won't pull a muscle. A few stretching exercises before going on the court are also valuable. On a very hot day, you'll find you'll warm up more quickly and be ready to go sooner. From five to seven minutes, depending on the temperature, is usually enough for a warm-up.

COMPETITION

Where does it all lead—all the things we've discussed about strokes, strategy, lessons, practice, conditioning and so forth? For many family players, tennis is an end in itself, something that's to be enjoyed for the fun, relaxation and exercise it provides. But others, with the incentive and the interest, will be eager to test themselves in tournament play.

Frankly, I believe everyone should experience some form of tennis competition. I realize that for every person who thrives on competition there is another person who is upset by it. Still, it seems to me that tennis competition will benefit every player no matter what his or her personality. Why? Because you learn a valuable lesson for life—you learn how to lose.

Competition is like an examination in school. It tells you how you stand, where you're strong, where you need to improve and something about what you are. There are all kinds of tennis competitions, some not so demanding as others.

Let's start with the junior level. All juniors should experience competition, starting as soon as they're eight years old. In competition between eight-year-olds, the word "choke" has never been heard. Tight situations don't bother them, so it's a perfect age to start. No doubt, some will be more aggressive than others, but the idea is to keep the competition simple. It can start with the very first lesson when the youngsters try to bounce the ball off the racquet —10 times down and 10 times up. That acts as an incentive to get the feel of the racquet. It's also competition—healthy competition. Then, they should go into other forms of competition, such as who will be the first to hit 10 serves in a row over the net. They're not competing against anyone in particular, just evaluating their own games. Finally, they come to the stage where they begin to compete against their peers, and it may be then you'll start

to see some temperament shown.

When facing a tournament, everyone—child or adult—should take the time to prepare for it. You should get your game as well as your body in shape. Jump rope, run and become used to being out in the sun if it's an outdoor event. I think the preparation for a social tournament is as important as the preparation for a professional tournament. I spend maybe two months getting ready for Wimbledon. So the social player can at least take a few days preparing for his club tournament.

As the competition begins, you're going to be geared up high, maybe too high to perform properly. To have maximum racquet control, you must be relaxed. I recall in the 1974 U.S. Open at Forest Hills when I was struggling in the first round with a player I should have beaten easily. I said to myself: "John, to win this tournament, you're going to have to have some fun. You're going to have to relax and enjoy seeing your combinations work and enjoy anticipating the results. You've got to laugh at yourself a little bit more if you make an error and get serious when the time comes to get serious." Once I started doing that, it was an easy victory.

Tension, you see, is something that's self-inflicted. Take the case of husbands and wives who play mixed doubles together. It often leads to problems. They're both all wound up trying to do their best—too much so. Spats and hurt feelings are often the result. My advice here is to relax, have a plan and simply play to the best of your ability.

Here are a few hints to relieve tension. Most people when they get nervous usually feel it in their legs. Others feel their breathing become short. When you feel tense, the first thing you should do is start to move. Did you ever notice how tension tends to evaporate when you're running or moving around a lot? So jump up and down a couple of times and get your feet in motion by taking little, short steps. If you feel short of breath, move your feet first and start to take deeper breaths through your diaphragm.

Another way to calm yourself down is to take a few practice swings just before serving or returning a serve. That will loosen up the stomach muscles. The next thing to do is to think positively. Over-play the ball, if anything, when you're feeling nervous. The natural tendency is to underplay it and shorten your follow-through. Give yourself plenty of room to hit. Instead of hitting the ball delicately, hit out more aggressively.

Tennis competition, you may notice, brings out the best as well as the worst in people. But it has important lessons for everyone. A little guy may be full of tears for 15 minutes after he loses, but from then on he's the happiest person you can find because he's experienced something. He's experienced a test; he's proved to himself that it's not as frightening as he thought and that he can handle it. He's also learned something about self-control.

You have to control yourself before you can control the ball, and you have to control the ball before you can control the match. I think one of the best features of tennis competition is that it teaches self-control.

FAMILY GOALS

Tennis, I feel, can and should be a healthy force in a family—something that fosters togetherness, enjoyment and exercise. The object should not be to produce champions. I know it isn't at Angie's and my house. It happens that we play well and have built our lives around the game. But the only real goal we have for our children is that they become good human beings.

If they take up tennis seriously, fine. All we ask is that they do their best and enjoy themselves. And that, I think, is all any tennis family can ask.

EXERCISES TO STAY IN SHAPE

*Exercise is the key to success. Jumping drills
like jack-knives (above) are excellent for
spring, legs and stomach. Stretching the leg
muscles regularly (right) will help prevent
muscle strains and pulls. The two photos at far
right show me doing a good stomach exercise.
The feet should not touch the ground. Legs
and stomach are the most important
things for a tennis player.*

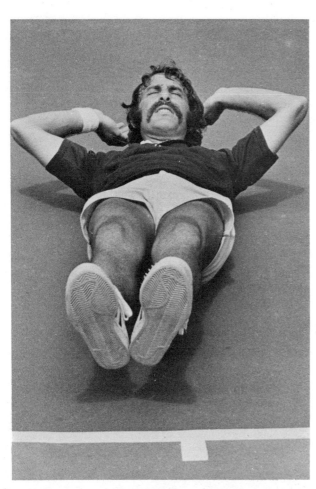

PRACTICE DRILLS

Serving from the service line, rather than the baseline (left), makes my serve fast enough to give John great practice on his return of serve. Two-on-one drills (below left) also help John keep sharp. The workout with his two students, Harrison Bowes (left) and Greg Houston (right) from Chicago, will help him with flexibility and mobility. Hitting volleys with a practice partner, as John and I are doing (below), is a good way to improve your racquet control and timing.

GETTING A GOOD COACH

If you want to be a good tennis player, get a good coach and teacher. Even a top tennis player needs the experienced eye of a coach from time to time. Here Coach Mabry is pointing out some of the things that have attracted his attention on the video tape. When I am having a problem Clarence and I often video tape it and then together we closely study the playback. Apart from other things, Clarence and I feel strongly that tennis and life should be fun.

IMPROVING YOUR SERVE

Coach Mabry demonstrates a drill to improve your ball toss that can be done either outside against a fence or inside against a wall. Just practice tossing the ball so it goes straight up the wall. This will give you proper positioning for your toss during the serve. Below, I'm demonstrating a drill we show beginners. It teaches them hand and ball coordination for the serve. I simply toss the ball up and then catch it with my right hand, just as though I were serving. My head has come down a fraction too soon and it would help if I didn't close my eyes.

GOOD COORDINATION
Sometimes Clarence bets me I can't serve the ball into the court blind-folded (right). As I am writing this caption, I'm saying I did! Our baby Gigi (above), 18 months, is starting to pick up racquets and balls. Pool is a great relaxer (top) and good for hand-eye coordination.

CLOWNING ON COURT

A big part of our playing tennis as a family is to relax and have fun with our children and close friends. El Bandito (below) and friend (right) like to clown. Clint (bottom) sure loves that ball box.

FUN ON THE RUN
One of my favorite diversions is catching the Frisbee off the diving board (above). I bet Coach Mabry was the instigator when Angie went over the fence (left). Pancho loves to run, as I do (right). The best way to clear a fuzzy mind (and also a great conditioner for tennis) is a three-mile jog.

ADDITIONAL PHOTO CREDITS
Asher Birnbaum, page 35
Braunfels Studio, pages 68-69, 153
Fran Delphia, page 130
Bruce Curtis, page 131

GIVE
THE FAMILY TENNIS BOOK
TO A WOMAN YOU KNOW

Would you like to share THE FAMILY TENNIS BOOK with someone you know? Ask for the book at your local bookstore. If for some reason the book should be unavailable, use the reverse side of this card to order directly from the publisher.

GIVE
THE FAMILY TENNIS BOOK
TO A MAN YOU KNOW

Would you like to share THE FAMILY TENNIS BOOK with someone you know? Ask for the book at your local bookstore. If for some reason the book should be unavailable, use the reverse side of this card to order directly from the publisher.

GIVE
THE FAMILY TENNIS BOOK
TO A CHILD YOU KNOW

Would you like to share THE FAMILY TENNIS BOOK with someone you know? Ask for the book at your local bookstore. If for some reason the book should be unavailable, use the reverse side of this card to order directly from the publisher.

GIVE
THE FAMILY TENNIS BOOK
TO A FAMILY YOU KNOW

Would you like to share THE FAMILY TENNIS BOOK with someone you know? Ask for the book at your local bookstore. If for some reason the book should be unavailable, use the reverse side of this card to order directly from the publisher.

Please send _____ copy(ies) of **THE FAMILY TENNIS BOOK** @ $4.95.
Include your check for the proper amount. Delacorte Press will pay
postage and handling charges. Add tax where applicable.

MAIL TO:
Delacorte Press
Box 2000
Pinebrook, N.J. 07056

Name_____

Address_____

City_____ **State**_____ **Zip**_____

Please send _____ copy(ies) of **THE FAMILY TENNIS BOOK** @ $4.95.
Include your check for the proper amount. Delacorte Press will pay
postage and handling charges. Add tax where applicable.

MAIL TO:
Delacorte Press
Box 2000
Pinebrook, N.J. 07056

Name_____

Address_____

City_____ **State**_____ **Zip**_____

Please send _____ copy(ies) of **THE FAMILY TENNIS BOOK** @ $4.95.
Include your check for the proper amount. Delacorte Press will pay
postage and handling charges. Add tax where applicable.

MAIL TO:
Delacorte Press
Box 2000
Pinebrook, N.J. 07056

Name_____

Address_____

City_____ **State**_____ **Zip**_____

Please send _____ copy(ies) of **THE FAMILY TENNIS BOOK** @ $4.95.
Include your check for the proper amount. Delacorte Press will pay
postage and handling charges. Add tax where applicable.

MAIL TO:
Delacorte Press
Box 2000
Pinebrook, N.J. 07056

Name_____

Address_____

City_____ **State**_____ **Zip**_____